KING & COLLECTOR

KING & COLLECTOR

Henry VIII and the Art of Kingship

LINDA COLLINS & SIOBHAN CLARKE

The History Press

Linda Collins: With thanks to my husband John for his invaluable support and endless cups of tea.

Siobhan Clarke: To my darling, Roger Pheby, for your encouragement and endurance of all things Henry.

First published 2021

The History Press
97 St George's Place, Cheltenham,
Gloucestershire, GL50 3QB
www.thehistorypress.co.uk

British Library Cataloguing in Publication Data.
A catalogue record for this book is available from the British Library.

ISBN 978 0 7509 9624 2

Typesetting and origination by The History Press
Printed in Turkey by Imak

CONTENTS

LIST OF ILLUSTRATIONS

FOREWORD

BY FLORIAN SCHWEIZER

Learning about the arts should always be an enriching and satisfying experience. Crucial to that experience are inspiring narrators who can breathe life into the stories of the past that are captured in art and material culture. It is a real joy to be in the presence of experts who not only understand their subject matter but also the audience they are sharing their knowledge with. Patricia Fay, the founder of The Arts Society, always insisted that learning should be enjoyable. This is still an ideal we aspire to in all we do at The Arts Society today, and in this book we find much that readers will enjoy.

Linda Collins and Siobhan Clarke bring a magnificent and dreadful king to life through the visual medium of his paintings, and in doing so create an impression of knowing the man more intimately. Henry VIII left a collection of not just valuable gold and jewels, but smaller and more personal items such as toothpicks and bandages for his legs.

Holbein's drawings of Henry's court create the cast of a Tudor play in which the twists and turns of the plot were often deadly. We can look into the faces of men and women whose last memory before facing the scaffold may well have been the cold and frigid eyes of King Henry himself.

To read this book is to become more personally acquainted with this tyrannical Tudor king through images of him painted by the people who knew him.

'The Art of Kingship' is indeed an apt subtitle for this little book that offers us an enormous visual slice of Henry's life. It is presented in a human context of which Patricia Fay would almost certainly have approved.

Florian Schweizer
CEO, The Arts Society

FOREWORD

BY BRETT DOLMAN

Back in 1537, when Hans Holbein the Younger put down his brushes and paints and stood back to admire his latest creation, he would not have known that his portrait of Henry VIII, full-size and confrontational, staring down from the wall of the Whitehall Palace Privy Chamber, would become the most iconic royal portrait in English history.

Holbein's Henry VIII is immediately recognisable to us as a statement of the unforgiving, brutish power of the Tudor dynasty. We can look through and beyond the portrait (with the benefit of hindsight and from the distant safety of the twenty-first century) to uncover the terror and magnificence of the Tudor age. We can glimpse the luxurious hubris, the paranoid authority and the unforgiving justice of Henry VIII's reign. Art reveals the past.

And Tudor art is more than just Holbein's portrait. The first half of the sixteenth century was a rich and revolutionary period when England attempted to embrace the Renaissance, enticing continental artists across the Channel to add cultural lustre and modernism to Henry's court. At the same time, teams of artists and craftsmen were employed on a startling range of artistic endeavours, from heraldic decoration to mural cycles celebrating the achievements of the Tudor monarchy.

This is a book about Tudor art, but also the stories within and around each artwork, from the history paintings that eulogised Henry VIII's early military campaigns in France through to the Abraham tapestries, commissioned towards the end of his reign, that were as much a vindication of the King's political and religious choices that shaped early modern England as they are stunning Renaissance artworks, still jewels in the Royal Collection and on display at Hampton Court Palace today.

In their account, the authors have succeeded where many others have failed. Art has not been reduced to mere illustration; it becomes an immersive gateway into an exploration of Tudor culture, political symbolism and spirituality. We also have a well-matched account of Henry himself – the nature of his kingship, his ambitions, achievements, failures, frustrations and insecurities – and we follow his path from ebullient masquer and triumphant jouster to the crippled, irascible tyrant. For Henry VIII, art was both an integral part of what has been called 'the swaggering theatre of court life' and a personal statement about his magnificence, sophistication and dynastic power. He commissioned, collected and consumed art.

From the audacious scale and ambition of the ephemeral architecture on display at the Field of Cloth of Gold to the exquisite quality and detail of English miniature portraiture, this book traces the dazzling range of artistic achievements of Henry VIII's reign, along with contextual and technical insights to help the reader navigate this very different visual world. Through the text and the artworks, we can glimpse a lost world of bejewelled courtiers and palaces drenched in the colour and symbolism of sixteenth-century art and craftsmanship, as well as understand what it meant to Henry VIII and the Tudor art of kingship.

Brett Dolman
Curator (Collections),
Historic Royal Palaces

INTRODUCTION

PICTURES AND PATTERNS OF A MERCILESS PRINCE

IF ALL THE PICTURES AND PATTERNS OF A MERCILESS PRINCE WERE LOST IN THE WORLD, THEY MIGHT ALL AGAIN BE PAINTED TO THE LIFE OUT OF THE STORY OF THIS KING

SIR WALTER RALEIGH

WHITEHALL PALACE, SPRING 1537. The assistants have stretched the drawing over the wall of the great privy chamber and pounced charcoal dust into holes they have pricked around the outline. Pigments and varnishes, purchased from London apothecaries, stand ready alongside an array of brushes, made from the hair of hogs and squirrels' tails.

A 40-year-old foreigner crosses the chamber casually; he is accustomed to the magnificence of gilded panelling, costly tapestries, shining tiled floors and brilliant moulded ceilings. He is extremely well dressed for an artist, but this is no ordinary craftsman. There is a hush as he removes his fur-collared gown, changes into a paint-stained doublet and starts to roll up his linen shirtsleeves.

Everyone stands back when the drawing is removed from the wall and the dots of charcoal left behind show the outline of a man, massive and menacing. Another hush. Hans Holbein is about to paint Henry VIII into history.

No English king is as well known to us as Henry VIII. He is famous for six marriages, for breaking with the Pope, dissolving the monasteries and creating the Church of England, and for his ruthless elimination of those who stood in his way. Between 1509 and 1547, more English notables were executed than under any other monarch before or since. But he was also an enthusiastic patron of the arts who established the most magnificent court ever seen in England.

No English monarch ever owned as many houses or spent so lavishly. His palaces, tapestries and paintings enriched the Tudor court and began the Royal Collection, but in contrast to later royal collectors, Henry was not interested in works of art or artists for their own sake. He was interested in storytelling through art, displaying his wealth, and promoting his own agenda.

'Art' is not a term that would have been recognised in early sixteenth-century England. An artist was simply a craftsman who shared the same status as a carpenter or a saddler and with an earning potential well below that of a goldsmith or silversmith. The whole concept of 'painting a painting' was alien in England. There was no 'art for art's sake' and the Italian idea of an artist being a 'genius' was almost unknown.

Most painters in this early Tudor age were employed in producing decorative work that would not have been intended to endure – signwriting, inn signs, banners, coats of arms and painted cloths. Artists employed at the royal court were required to produce stage scenery for court masques and heraldic emblems within the palaces. Even decorating the royal barge would have been included in their job specification. Due to its ephemeral nature, only a small amount of this kind of production is left to us.

Later in the Tudor period, art began to appear in public spaces, in town halls and livery companies, and in domestic homes; to own a portrait of the monarch was to show allegiance to the Crown. In a century rife with theological dispute, pictures of people tended to survive where overtly religious works did not, but even a conservative estimate assumes that 40 per cent of the portraits produced in the reign of Henry VIII are lost. We should therefore be aware that we are judging the genre on what we have left, rather than on what was produced within its time.

Before 1540 the majority of portraits commissioned were of royalty or the aristocracy, but from then onwards the merchant classes began to contract with artists to produce painted images. This has something to do with affluence, but it was also a leap in self-confidence. In only one generation, families advanced to the point where they wanted and were able to imitate the fashions of the royal court.

In his pursuit of glory and magnificence, Henry VIII has left us with a collection that has continued to grow. Until the Civil War and the execution of Charles I – during which many works were put up for sale – the Royal Collection that Henry founded was the equal of any great collection in Europe. Today, it comprises over 1 million objects including more than 7,000 paintings and over 2,000 tapestries, plates, engravings, books, clocks and furniture.

Those objects acquired by Henry VIII tell the story of his life and reign. It is the story of a boy who was not expected to become king and who grew into a man yearning to show off his prowess in warfare. In *The Battle of the Spurs* we see a young king, in his early 20s, impatient to fight. Seven years later in the large picture *The Field of the Cloth of Gold* Henry is learning the art of diplomacy. *A Protestant Allegory* presents Henry's version of the break from Rome, and the Whitehall Mural shows us an intimidating king at the height of his power who has defied the Pope. The art of miniature painting became popular in Henry's reign and, with the arrival of Hans Holbein the Younger, the fashion for portraiture began. In his search for a fourth queen, Henry chose Anne of Cleves on the strength of a portrait by Holbein, although he later regretted his decision. These images still have the power to bewitch centuries later, though for different reasons. There is a fascination with portraiture in general that may stem from the ability to look at the face of a person who was alive in the past. We can know the excitement of looking at someone who looked into the eyes of Henry VIII. The glorious Abraham tapestries embody the splendour and propaganda of the Tudor dynasty and *The Family of Henry VIII*, set in a sumptuous Whitehall Palace, portrays an older Henry, presiding over his dynasty and its secure continuation. Finally, an engraving of the king in old age, by Cornelis Metsys, shows us a man in decline, but a man who to the end employed magnificence as a symbol of his authority.

The life of Henry VIII – his passion and power – can be seen through his art collection. The paintings he commissioned tell us much about his kingship and (unintentionally) his insecurities. Ultimately, each of the works told some aspect of one central story: the glorification of Henry and his England.

I

FATHER AND SON: HENRY VII AND HENRY VIII

THE GREAT DEBATE, COMPETITION AND GREAT QUESTION IS WHETHER FATHER OR SON IS THE VICTOR.
FOR BOTH, INDEED, WERE SUPREME

WHITEHALL MURAL

HENRY VIII WAS BORN at Greenwich on 28 June 1491, the second son of Henry VII and Elizabeth of York. He passed his early years happily at Eltham Palace, playing in the royal nursery with his sisters and learning his letters from his mother. The young prince would grow up tutored in both the rationalism of the new humanist learning and the romance of medieval chivalry. He read Jean Froissart's *Chronicles* and Sir Thomas Malory's *Le Morte Darthur* with his first tutor, the poet John Skelton; stories which glorified personal combat and the pure code of honour for all true knights. This code would be crucial to Henry's sense of self for the rest of his life. Unsurprisingly, his favourite personal hero was Henry V, the English king who vanquished the French at Agincourt in 1415.

Henry saw little of his brother, Arthur, who was five years his senior. Upon Arthur's sudden death in 1502, Henry became heir to the throne and went to live at court with his father. According to chroniclers, the king underwent a change of character in his later years: he became more secretive and avaricious, extracting money from his subjects through bonds and fines. His behaviour became erratic, with long bouts of illness and sudden rages, and his relationship with young Henry was distant.

English history is full of conflicts between the monarch and the heir to the throne. The prince who took Arthur's place was a boisterous youth, highly educated and athletic, who looked like his Yorkist ancestors. We are given an insight into the outgoing temperament of Henry VIII as a child by Desiderius Erasmus, who met him at Eltham Palace in the company of fellow humanist writer Sir Thomas More:

> In the midst stood prince Henry, then nine years old, and having already something of royalty in his demeanour, in which there was a certain dignity combined with singular courtesy. More … presented [Henry] with some writing. For my part, not having expected anything of the sort, I had nothing to offer, but promised that on another occasion I would in some way declare my duty towards him. Meanwhile I was angry with More for not having warned me, especially as the boy sent me a little note, while we were at dinner, to challenge something from my pen.

However, in the company of Henry VII, the boy seems to have been more subdued. It may have come as a shock to find that life at his father's court was very restrictive. He was closely monitored and protected by bodyguards, his movements limited even within the palaces. The Spanish Ambassador described him as 'so subjected that he does not speak a word except in response to what the king asks him'. Henry VII may have feared that discontented elements might make his son a figurehead for rebellion; or perhaps he was simply being overprotective of his only surviving male heir. Over thirty years later, Henry VIII would make clear the relationship between father and son in the Whitehall Mural, with a statement in the Latin inscription: 'The great debate, competition and great question is whether father or son is the victor. For both, indeed, were supreme.'

Henry VII had used painters, stonemasons, illuminators, poets and historians to project himself as the legitimate King of England through regal image-making. His claim to royal blood was tenuous, derived from his mother Margaret Beaufort, who was descended from Edward III. Henry Tudor had taken the crown by force in 1485, after defeating Richard III at Bosworth Field. His subsequent marriage to King Richard's niece Elizabeth of York had done much to heal his war-torn kingdom, but there were still discontented elements and rivals to his throne. The new Tudor king needed propaganda to bolster his position. He understood that the illusion of power and wealth was as important as the real thing and was prepared to spend lavish amounts on royal palaces and tapestries. Portraits were mainly commissioned for display at court or for diplomatic purposes. Henry VII's use of them differed little from that of his immediate predecessors, the Plantagenet Houses of York and Lancaster, who produced portraits to send to foreign courts or to advertise themselves in the marriage market. Images of the king might also be placed within a religious setting, to emphasise how his position was legitimised by his relationship with God and the Church; for example, in *The Family of Henry VII with St George and the Dragon*.

The Family of Henry VII with St George and the Dragon

Flemish school, c. 1503–09, oil on panel, Royal Collection Trust

The story of St George varies, but the most popular version is told in Jacobus de Voragine's *Golden Legend*, written in 1292. Voragine was a Dominican chronicler who became Archbishop of Genoa. The scene takes place in a small settlement in Libya, represented in the painting by the exotic towers in the background. A fearful dragon occupied a lake in Silene and threatened to enter and destroy the town, looking for food. To prevent this, every day the dragon was provided with a sheep. When all the sheep in the area had been consumed it was decreed the creature should be fed a child. Lots were drawn to select the unlucky victim.

One day, the short straw was chosen by the king, who was expected to give up his daughter, the beautiful Princess Cleodoline. He offered all his gold in her place, but the townspeople refused so the maiden was clothed in regal finery and led towards her death. The lamb with her, in the painting, represents the sacrificial lamb, suggestive of martyrdom. Just as she was about to be fed to the dragon, St George witnessed her plight and pierced the monster's neck with his lance – but he stopped short of killing it and tied it to a tree instead. Turning to the people

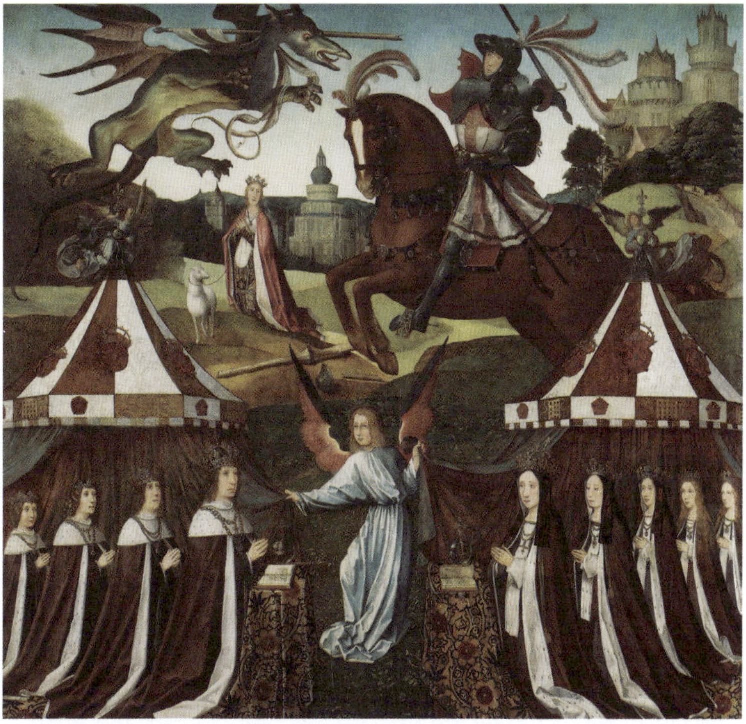

The Family of Henry VII with St George and the Dragon.
Probably an altarpiece, possibly for Richmond Palace.

of the town, George told them that if they converted to Christianity then he would save them from further bloodshed. When the whole town pledged to convert, St George slayed the dragon.

In most paintings of St George and the dragon, the creature is pictured on the ground with St George towering above him. However, in this version, the two adversaries are facing each other. They are eye-to-eye and – unusually – the dragon is slightly higher than St George. A broken lance lies discarded on the ground; clearly, the battle is not yet won.

St George was patron saint of England and one of the three saints of the Order of the Garter, a group of honourable knights. Tudor roses abound in this composition, and the resemblance between St George, protector of England, and King Henry VII, defender of his land and people, would not have been missed by the contemporary viewer.

In the lower half of the painting two campaign tents are held aloft by tiny angels. Tudor roses again decorate the tents, along with the portcullis, the symbol of Henry's mother, Margaret Beaufort. Within the tents are the family of Henry VII, the males on one side and the females on the other. A larger angel grasps the flaps of the tents in each of his hands, visually uniting the family.

The scene is a reminder of the fragility of life. Henry VII died soon after the painting was completed, and of the princes kneeling behind him only Prince Henry was still living. His older brother, Arthur, had been dead for seven years and his youngest brother, Edmund, had passed away at only a year old. On the female side, Henry's queen, Elizabeth of York, died following the birth of their daughter Catherine in 1503. Two of the princesses were still living, but two of them, Elizabeth and Catherine, had died as babies.

The children who died in infancy have been painted into the picture as if they had lived. The Tudor dynasty was in its early days and the need for a fruitful marriage with a large family and a string of healthy male heirs and beautiful princess brides was required to reinforce a message of strength and continuity. The painting may have been intended as an altarpiece for Richmond Palace, but there are no signs that it had adjoining wings, which would make it an extremely early example in England of a single panel altarpiece. More likely, it would have been placed on a wall behind the altar.

EARLY PORTRAITS

The Tudors were possibly the first English rulers whose faces were familiar to their subjects, and Henry VIII's desire to be regarded as a European monarch led to his image being disseminated far more widely than that of his predecessors.

The term 'portrait' was unknown and painted images were referred to as a 'counterfeit' or a 'duplication' because they copied the image of a person who was absent. Every portrait in early Tudor England was painted for a specific occasion – to display wealth, power and status or to mark an important event in the life of the sitter. There was no concept in England that art could be purchased purely as decoration for the home. Portraits of men dominated the genre; there were fewer pictures of women and fewer still of children.

Henry VII

Unknown Netherlandish artist, 1505, oil on panel, National Portrait Gallery

Portraits of Henry VII, Elizabeth of York and their daughter Margaret Tudor were sent to James IV in 1502, during negotiations for Margaret's marriage with the Scottish king. Three years later, an unknown Flemish artist completed an impressive and lifelike portrait of Henry VII, now a widower. The inscription confirms that the portrait was painted on 29 October 1505 on the order of Herman Rinck, an agent of the Holy Roman Emperor, Maximilian. It was part of Henry's attempt to marry Maximilian's daughter, Margaret of Savoy, as his second wife.

Margaret of Savoy's life had been turbulent. Her mother died when she was just 2 years old and, having made an alliance with Louis XI, her father sent her to live at the French court, to be raised as a future Queen of France. However, she was returned to Burgundy aged 13 and, four years later, she married Prince Juan of Spain. It was a union marred by tragedy. Margaret appears to have loved her husband, but he died after just six months and their first child was stillborn. She married again, aged 21, to Philibert, Duke of Savoy, but within three years, he too died, leaving her childless. Not surprisingly, she vowed never to marry again. Her court in Mechelen, a city between Brussels and Antwerp, gained a reputation for education and elegance. Anne Boleyn, Henry VIII's second wife, would later spend time there before moving to the French court. It is against this background that the 25-year-old Margaret of Savoy was asked to consider Henry VII as a potential husband.

King Henry, now 48, had lost his eldest son three years before and his wife had died following childbirth. We are

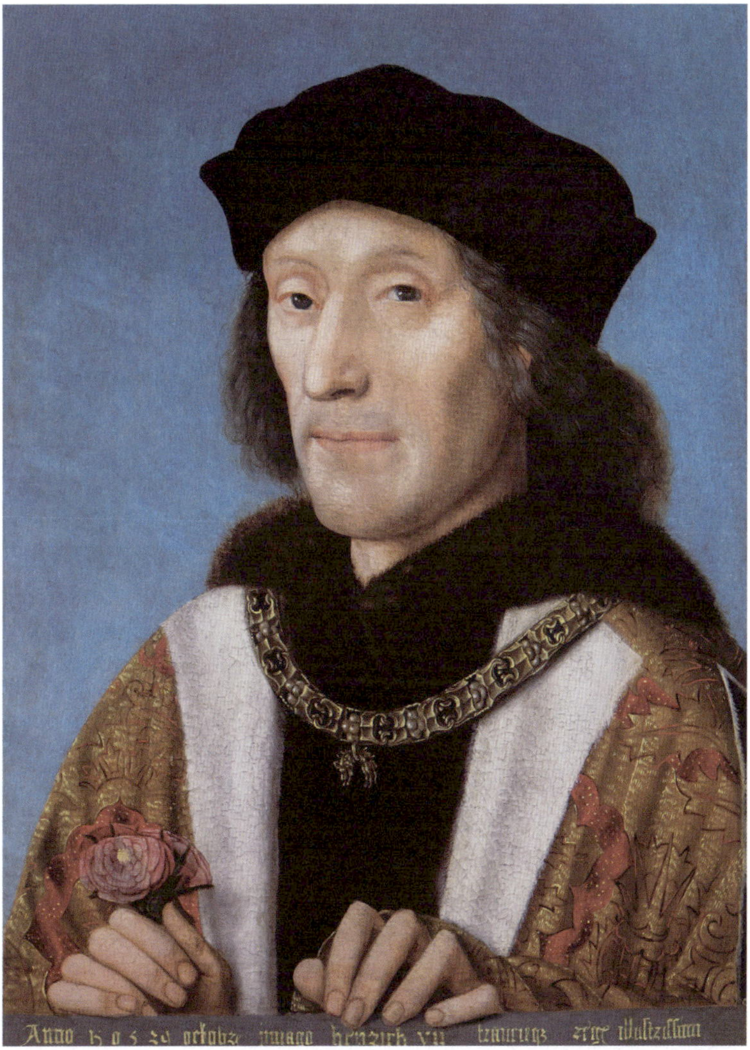

This portrait of Henry VII by a Netherlandish artist dates from 1505 and is the earliest painting in the National Portrait Gallery's collection.

looking at a man in mourning, but also at a king searching for a political alliance to strengthen his rule and his country.

The position of the hands, resting on the frame within the picture, is not innovative but rather part of an established tradition. The novelty of the portrait lies in its frankness. It is an unusually honest depiction of an elderly man. The lack of flattery suggests that it may have been painted from life, something royal sitters might allow only two or three times during their reign. More commonly, patterns were used by artists to gain a lifelike image at a time when many had not seen the king and only knew his features from coins and medals.

His is not an attractive face. Although the eyes are alert, the angle of the eyelids suggests a certain slyness. His lips are thin and set into what could be interpreted as a smile – or a smirk. Instead of wearing the insignia of the English Order of the Garter, he is painted wearing the Burgundian Order of the Golden Fleece because it was more easily recognised and influential abroad. Henry VII was elected to this order in 1491, the year his son Henry was born. And so, there is intention, but seemingly no physical artifice in this portrait.

The king has chosen to be painted wearing a black cap, a black and dark red tunic and a surcoat made of red brocade trimmed with white fur. The red rose that he holds is associated with the house of Lancaster but, in this context, it could also represent the love and friendship that Henry wishes to offer a potential bride.

The artist is unknown but we can guess his nationality from the gold jewellery and regalia of the Order of the Golden Fleece, which are skilfully and carefully reproduced – a speciality of Flemish artists in this early period. There may have been more than one artist at work because, by comparison, the eyes look dull. It could have been produced by a Netherlandish artist residing in London or by a painter chosen by Maximilian to travel to England specifically for the purpose. Given the varied quality of the piece, the former is more likely.

The panel is oak and the frame is an integral part of the picture, meaning both the panel and the frame were carved from one piece of wood with the arched element added and gilded. An inventory of 1516 suggests that the painting may have had a red cover that would have been nailed to the frame, perhaps to secure it for travelling or storing, as nails can still be seen by infrared technology.

In the end, Margaret of Savoy made her choice and rejected Henry as her third husband; presumably not impressed with this image of him as a potential suitor. Now it hangs in the National Portrait Gallery in London, the earliest painting in the collection.

In contrast to the extremely high cost of tapestries and the luxury textiles used for court dress, portraits were relatively inexpensive in England. Artists had the status of artisans and would not have charged as much as expert tapestry weavers. Henry VII established royal workshops for artists and skilled workmen, who took on many different types of commissions from designing jewellery to domestic interiors and banners. Artists were certainly not celebrities; there was no English school of painting and hardly any signed their work. The English didn't even use the word 'painting'; they called an image painted on an oak panel a 'table'; if painted on canvas, it was a 'cloth'.

A generation before the reign of Henry VIII, the court's artistic inspiration came from Burgundy – which had a huge cultural influence – with just a few examples of

Renaissance art such as the Italian Guido Mazzoni's bust of a smiling boy.

HENRY VIII WHEN A YOUNG BOY (?)

Guido Mazzoni, (d. 1518), 1498, painted and gilded terracotta, Royal Collection Trust

It is a fragile work that has been part of the Royal Collection since 1498. There is mention of the piece in the seventeenth century, during the reign of James II, when it appeared in an inventory at Whitehall Palace as *Head of a Laughing Boy*, but frustratingly there is no record of how or why it came into the collection. It is a famous and popular object because so few images of the young Henry VIII survive. Could this be one of them?

In 1925, the Surveyor of the King's Pictures, Lionel Cust, attributed the piece to the sculptor Guido Mazzoni, nicknamed Paganino or Modanino. Mazzoni was from Modena, a city in Northern Italy that was ruled by the House of Este, famously a family of art patrons. He was brought up by his uncle, who was an official for the Este Government, and it may have been through him that, aged around 23, Mazzoni won his first commission to sculpt festival masks for the wedding of Ercole d'Este, Duke of Ferrara, to Eleanor of Naples in 1473.

Mazzoni evolved to become a master of coloured, life-size statues. These were principally of religious figures that formed tableaux in churches; his most celebrated work is a *Lamentation* in the Church of Gésu in Ferrara. They were not sculpted in the usual stone or marble but in terracotta, which was more freely available and much cheaper. Over the centuries, this choice of material has

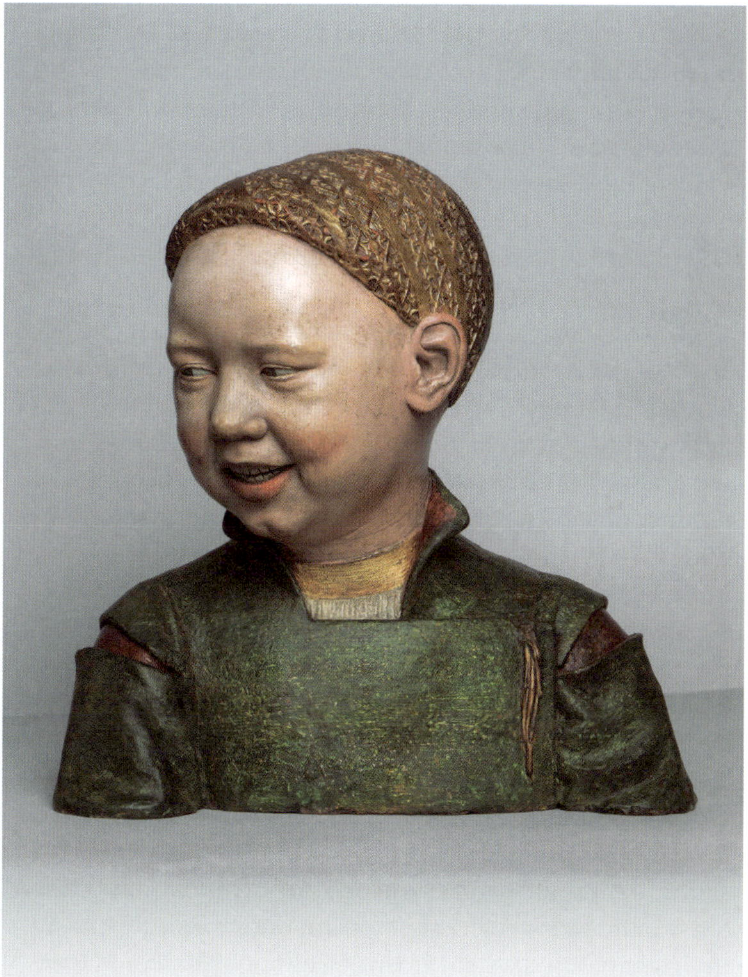

A painted and gilded terracotta sculpture by Guido Mazzoni. It has been described as a portrait of Henry VIII as a 7-year-old boy.

perhaps limited Mazzoni's fame as a sculptor. Terracotta is particularly prone to natural disintegration and was also viewed as a poor relation to bronze or marble, meaning that sculptures in terracotta were often discounted as provincial. It is Mazzoni's astonishingly detailed observation of human characteristics, his technical skill and his natural colouring that brings the figures to life and associates him with this sculpture of a young boy.

The terracotta used in sculpting this bust is exceptionally thin, only 5mm, so it would have been easily broken. The unusual pose would have also presented a challenge to the artist. An open-mouthed smile is rare in both painting and sculpture because it is difficult for the artist to produce and even more difficult for the sitter to maintain without it turning into an unattractive grimace. However, in this case the smile serves a purpose. During the firing, steam must escape from the sculpture in order to prevent the terracotta shattering in the kiln. Along with the two earholes, the open mouth would have provided a vent for excess moisture. At the time of firing this cheeky-looking boy would literally have had steam coming out of his ears and mouth.

In 1985, some overpainting was removed from the sculpture, revealing that the original composition of the boy's tunic was a layer of tin foil cut out into a pattern and then overpainted with a green glaze. The light would have played on the surface and created a richness that was most likely meant to imitate cloth of gold, a material woven from threads of pure gold (the earliest example of cloth of gold in England can be seen in the *Wilton Diptych* in the National Gallery, London, dated *c.* 1395). Cloth of gold was expensive to produce and few people outside the church or royalty would have been able to afford it. However, it was certainly within the means of a young Prince Henry.

There is no record of Mazzoni coming to London, but he did leave his native Modena to accept employment at the court of Charles VIII in France and during his time there he submitted a design for the tomb of Henry VII. Mazzoni's design was dismissed in favour of one by a fellow Italian, Torrigiano, but perhaps the sculpture accompanied the design on the way to England as an example of the artist's skill?

Prince Henry was aged 7 when the piece was sculpted and it is on this basis that the work has been attributed. It is an intriguing puzzle, because if it is not Prince Henry then who could it have been? Arthur, Prince of Wales, can be ruled out. He was nearing 12 and was thinner and finer boned than the more rounded Henry. Mazzoni was working for Charles VIII at the time, but the children of the French king predeceased him at early ages, certainly before reaching the age of 7. Perhaps it shows a member of the wealthy Este family, former patrons of Mazzoni? But the image of an Italian prince is unlikely to have been thought a relevant gift for King Henry VII.

The sculpture has guarded its secrets well. Over the years it has been described as a Chinese boy, a laughing girl, a German dwarf and a portrait of Henry VIII as a 7-year-old boy. Until further research identifies the subject with certainty, the attribution to Prince Henry must remain disappointingly and tantalisingly conjectural.

THE RENAISSANCE IN ENGLAND

Henry VII's plans to marry Margaret of Savoy and beget more heirs never came to fruition. He died of tuberculosis at Richmond Palace in April 1509. The Tudor matriarch, Margaret Beaufort, followed her son to the grave just two months later. The new king, Henry VIII, declared that he would marry Katherine of Aragon, his brother's widow, and they were crowned together within two months of his succession. Young Henry was hailed as the embodiment of a Renaissance prince: cultured, noble, strong and vigorous. A contemporary observer described him thus: 'he speaks good French, Latin and Spanish; is very religious; heard three masses daily ... He is extremely fond of hunting, and never takes that diversion without tiring eight or ten horses ... He is also fond of tennis.' Henry wanted to rule justly and to dazzle everyone with his splendid court; he promised peace in England, but he also craved military triumph abroad. His foreign policy was aimed at reviving the glory days of Henry V and the chivalry of Camelot. William Blount, Lord Mountjoy, was clearly impressed: 'what a hero now shows himself, how wisely he behaves, what a lover he is of justice and goodness ... all the world here is rejoicing in the possession of so great a prince ...'

Above all, the young Henry VIII was an enlightened monarch, eager to rival other European rulers not only in war, but in magnificence and the arts. It would be his patronage, and the European artists he imported, which would properly bring the Renaissance to England. Royal agents were sent abroad to recruit these talented artists and soon the finest artists and craftsmen working in England were foreigners.

The first great Italian employed by Henry VIII was the sculptor Pietro Torrigiano, a superbly talented man who had studied alongside Michelangelo in Florence. In the cultural backwater of England, he would design and execute a tomb for Henry VII and Elizabeth of York that would be considered his masterpiece.

Tomb of Henry VII and Elizabeth of York

Pietro Torrigiano (1472–1528), 1509, black marble and copper gilt, Lady Chapel, Westminster Abbey

'Here is situated Henry VII, the glory of all kings who lived in his time by reason of his intellect, his riches and the fame of his exploits.' This is the inscription, translated from Latin, on the tomb of Henry VII and Elizabeth of York in the Lady Chapel in Westminster Abbey. The inscription continues, 'Joined to him his sweet wife was very pretty, chaste and fruitful. They were parents happy in their offspring, to whom, land of England, you owe Henry VIII'.

Torrigiano arrived in England sometime before 1511, the year he was paid £1,500 to design and produce the tomb of Henry VII and Elizabeth of York. Indentures of the works still exist; Torrigiano's name must have proved difficult to spell because he is listed as 'Peter Torrysany'. He lived in the precincts of St Peter's, Westminster, while working on the tomb, and although his furious temper was legendary, there are no known records of disputes when he was in England. The tomb was not completed until 1517 – eight years after Henry VIII became king. Torrigiano had asked another Italian, Benvenuto Cellini, to assist him, but Cellini refused to work with a man of such violent temper, nor did he wish to live among 'such beasts as the English'.

Torrigiano's most famous misdeed – and perhaps the reason he was in England – was his fight with Michelangelo in which he broke the younger sculptor's nose. In his autobiography, Cellini remembers that Torrigiano said he 'felt bone and cartilage go down like biscuit beneath my knuckles and this mark of mine he will carry with him to the grave'. Images of Michelangelo confirm this to be true. The conflict took place in the Carmine Church in Florence, when both artists were training at the Medici Academy. Michelangelo appears to have had an annoying habit of looking over the shoulders of other artists and making disparaging comments. We cannot be sure if this prompted the quarrel but, whatever the cause, Torrigiano's subsequent disgrace resulted in his departure from Florence.

In the medieval setting of Westminster Abbey, Torrigiano produced the first masterwork of Renaissance sculpture in England: Henry VII and Elizabeth of York cast in lifelike bronze effigies. They are shown reclining full length on a black marble tomb base, decorated with copper medallions of the Virgin Mary and twelve of Henry's patron saints, including St George and John the Baptist. The faces of the couple, which were made with the aid of death masks, are sensitively sculpted but still in the traditional gothic style. It is in the ornate tomb decoration that the influence of the Renaissance is most apparent. The angels at the corners are lively; they balance on the edges of the monument, looking as if they could move – and at one time there would have been movement because they were holding pennants in their hands that trembled in any breeze. At each end of the tomb are coats of arms supported by cherubs. The scheme originally included an elaborate altar at the head of the tomb but it was destroyed by Puritans, under the Commonwealth, in 1641.

Henry VII had asked that his funeral be performed without 'dampnable pompe and oterageous superluities' – in other words, in a simple fashion. This is most likely why he rejected a design by Guido Mazzoni, which incorporated two separate figures of the king, one reclining next to his wife while the second knelt

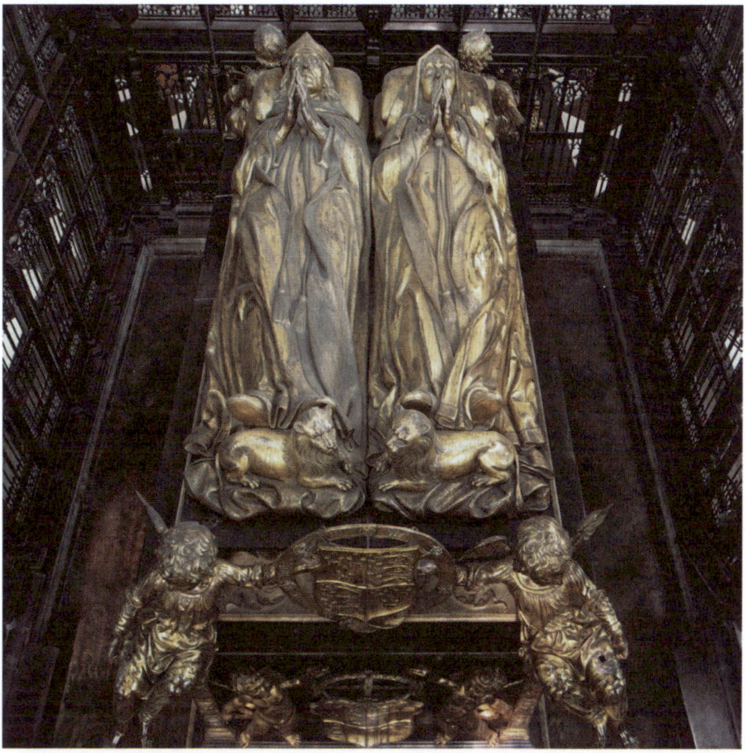

Torrigiano's tomb monument of Henry VII and Elizabeth of York in the Lady Chapel of Westminster Abbey.

on top of the tomb holding a crown. This was possibly to represent the king as the body politic and the body mortal in a similar fashion to the tomb that Mazzoni had produced for Charles VIII of France. It is clear that the less complicated design by Torrigiano was much closer to the will of Henry VII.

The existing grille surrounding the tomb was made by Thomas Ducheman (The Dutchman). The indentures for the work in the Lady Chapel date to 16 July 1504 and call for 'a closure of metal in manner of a chapel'. Onlookers would have seen the full splendour of the sepulchre newly gilded and supporting candles of almost 3m high that were lit on special anniversaries. In the cool and relative gloom of the chapel four additional candles burnt constantly, tended by monks.

Torrigiano was also asked to create a tomb for Henry VIII at Windsor, intended to be one fourth larger than that of his parents. Whether this design was to accommodate the taller and more muscular body of Henry VIII or to glorify him by comparison with his father is unknown because the tomb was never completed. The artist left England for Spain and abandoned the project. Unfortunately, Torrigiano's temper once again made an appearance and following a dispute over payment with the Duke of Arcus he smashed a marble sculpture he had made of the Virgin Mary. The Duke denounced him as a heretic, and he was arrested by the Inquisition and thrown into prison, where he ended his life by hunger strike in 1528 at the age of 55.

LATER PORTRAITS

England became a land of opportunity for artists under the young Henry VIII. The early part of the century saw the arrival of many craftsmen and talented painters from Germany and the Low Countries, as well as a few from Italy. Following the Protestant Reformation of the church, there was virtually no market for religious images in England, so most surviving painted images from this period are in the form of portraiture. Foreign painters complained that English patrons only cared for portraiture and rarely commissioned still life or history painting.

Portraits became increasingly fashionable for the elite, marking rites of passage such as marriage, death, the conferring of honours or a new political post. For example, Thomas Cromwell commissioned his portrait when he was appointed Master of the King's Jewel House in 1532. The sitters are often identified by badges, coats of arms and inscriptions, their rank and wealth proclaimed through dress, jewellery and insignia. They could be produced in multiple copies, which today can cause confusion over which is the original. They were important as a way of demonstrating status, wealth and power, while ownership of the king's portrait showed loyalty to the Crown, especially after his break with the Pope. Full-length portraits were rare; most were head-and-shoulders studies, painted to order and still considered to be of much less value than wall hangings. There were, however, paintings in the Royal Collection that were important – as dynastic advertisements and objects of glorification. We know something of Henry VIII's collection because inventories of his pictures were drawn up in 1542 and 1547. Twenty paintings hung in the galleries at Hampton Court in 1547, and 169 were hung at Whitehall Palace. We will turn to some of these important paintings later.

2

FROM WAR TO DIPLOMACY: THE EARLY YEARS

War is sweet to those who have never experienced it.

Desiderius Erasmus

When Henry VIII was crowned king at 18 years old, he could joust, hunt and dance the night away, but the ultimate test of his physical capabilities would come in battle – and the young Henry was eager to go to war to show off his prowess.

He matched himself with the great princes of Europe although his England comprised only 2 million people; a third of the population of Spain and a sixth of that of France. He dreamed of ruling France, and to this end he joined an alliance with the Pope, the Emperor Maximilian, and his father-in-law, Ferdinand of Aragon. In the summer of 1513, Henry invaded France with a force exceeding 30,000. His troops defeated a French army at the Battle of the Spurs in August – a relatively minor skirmish – and the following month the English took Thérouanne and Tournai, the latter a substantial centre of trade. The conquest marked Henry out as a force in European politics, but the territory was far inland and would be too expensive to maintain. These campaigns gave Henry a taste of military success. However, the war cost him a million pounds, consuming the personal fortune he had inherited from his father and driving up taxes.

Henry's absence from the country had prompted James IV of Scotland, allied to the French, to invade England in September 1513. The resulting battle left a whole generation of the Scottish nobility, and the Scottish king himself, dead on Flodden Field; it was a resounding English victory for Queen Katherine, whom Henry had left behind as governor of the realm. It would never be celebrated in art; such a victory would not register in Europe, nor in Henry's imagination as his victories in France did. In any case, Henry himself was not there!

The Battle of the Spurs

Flemish school, c. 1513, oil on canvas, Royal Collection Trust

The Battle of the Spurs took place on 16 August 1513 in what was described as 'foul weather'. The flat landscape is the north of France and the town on the hill is Thérouanne, situated today in the Nord-Pas-de-Calais region. The English troops are under the personal leadership of Henry VIII and the Imperial forces are under the command of Maximilian, Holy Roman Emperor. They have the town of Thérouanne under siege and are waiting

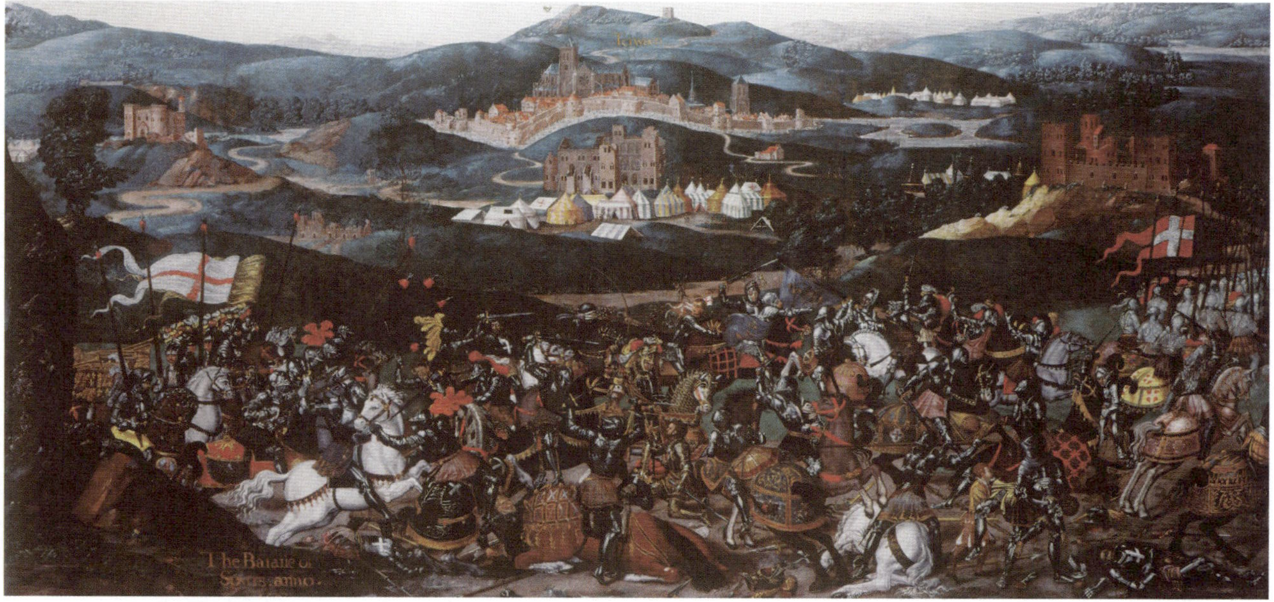

Henry's early military triumph over the French at Thérouanne, Northern France.
It was said the French 'used their spurs more than their swords'.

for its townsfolk to surrender – principally through lack of food. It is dawn and the French hope that by moving early they will catch the English unprepared and be able to bring provisions to the town. With this aim, each French light cavalry rider is equipped with a sack of gunpowder attached to the saddle behind him and a side of bacon with his saddlebow. But the English see them arrive and act swiftly; soon the French light cavalry is surrounded. They have been fired at by cannon and shot at from the hedgerows by English archers; they now find themselves hugely outnumbered and face to face with the might of the Imperial cavalry.

The commander of Louis XII's French forces, Jacques de la Palice, tries to rally his troops but panic has set in. Lances are discarded, standards are dropped in the field and the whole chaotic skirmish turns into a rout. The chase lasts for a couple of miles as the English follow in pursuit, gathering the dropped French standards for themselves and taking some high-ranking Frenchmen hostage for ransom. The title of the painting is thus explained: the French had ridden away so hard and furiously that the last view the English troops had of them was the sun glinting on their spurs as they rode into the distance. It has also been suggested that the French used their spurs far more than their swords and, in France, the battle became known as *La Journée d'Esperon* (Day of the Spurs). Within a few weeks of the conflict, the town of Thérouanne fell under English control.

Henry was present at the battle site but he had no heir, so it was essential to the kingdom and to the Tudor dynasty that he was kept far from danger. In this painting we see him wearing shining gilded armour and a helmet dressed with distinctive gold, blue and white feathers. He is seated on a white horse at the centre of the combat, his visor raised and his face revealed. Of course, this was not a truthful account. He was certainly there, but not in the heat of the fighting because his Privy Council ensured he was kept safely behind the front line.

Kneeling in front of Henry is a well-dressed officer, gesturing to the king as though in polite conversation. This man is a French nobleman, Pierre Terrail, Seigneur de Bayard. He is around 40, and to the 22-year-old Henry must have seemed positively ancient. But Terrail had a charming presence. His motto, *'le chevalier sans peur et sans reproche'* ('The knight without fear and beyond reproach') sums him up admirably.

Bayard had found himself cut off from the battlefield and it is easy to imagine this man of middle age being exhausted from physical exertion. In the past year he had fought both in the Siege of Brescia and the Battle of Ravenna. His morale was low, he was tired and he wanted no more of death and destruction. When he realised his escape route was cut off, Bayard rode up to a resting and unarmed English soldier and, putting his sword to the soldier's throat, ordered 'Surrender!' The unarmed English soldier, presumably shocked by Bayard's sudden apparition complied. Imagine his surprise when Bayard told him, 'Not you – me! I want to surrender'. And so, Bayard was taken into the English camp as a prisoner.

Bayard's gallantry and reputation impressed Henry VIII, who ordered that he be freed without ransom on condition that he agreed not to fight against the English for six weeks. Bayard was deprived of his sword and escorted from the field. With chivalric grace, however, it was stipulated that, should Bayard be attacked at any time before his release, his weapon would be returned to him, allowing him to defend himself.

The picture may not tell the truth in some respects, but it brutally reveals the anguish of war. To the right is a small, unprotected pageboy helping to carry the body of a soldier from the field. The armoured helmet in the forefront of the picture is likely to contain a head and the gauntlet facing towards the viewer possibly still encloses a hand. Battle was bloody and not always, if ever, glorious. Given the weapons available to them, these soldiers did not generally die quickly; they would have lain in agony from horrific injuries while the battle continued around them. As Erasmus wrote: 'War is sweet to those who have never experienced it.'

ARMOUR

The spectacular armour that Henry VIII is wearing in *The Battle of the Spurs* did not survive, but it was almost certainly made by foreign armourers. At this time, few English craftsmen could produce the fine-quality armour required by Henry and his court. The most important areas of production were in Northern Italy, particularly Milan, or in Southern Germany, from where England imported costly and elaborate arms and armour.

A suit of armour was closely fitted to the wearer and can provide an estimate of the wearer's height and shape to a margin of around 2.5–3.5cm. Henry's armour confirms his height was around 1.88cm (6ft 2in), which was tall for the time, with an 87.8cm waist (34.7in) and a chest measurement of 105.5cm (41.7in). As it was impractical for Henry to travel to Germany or to cross the Alps to Italy to be measured in person, his doublet and hose would, rather bizarrely, have been sent abroad as a guide to his shape.

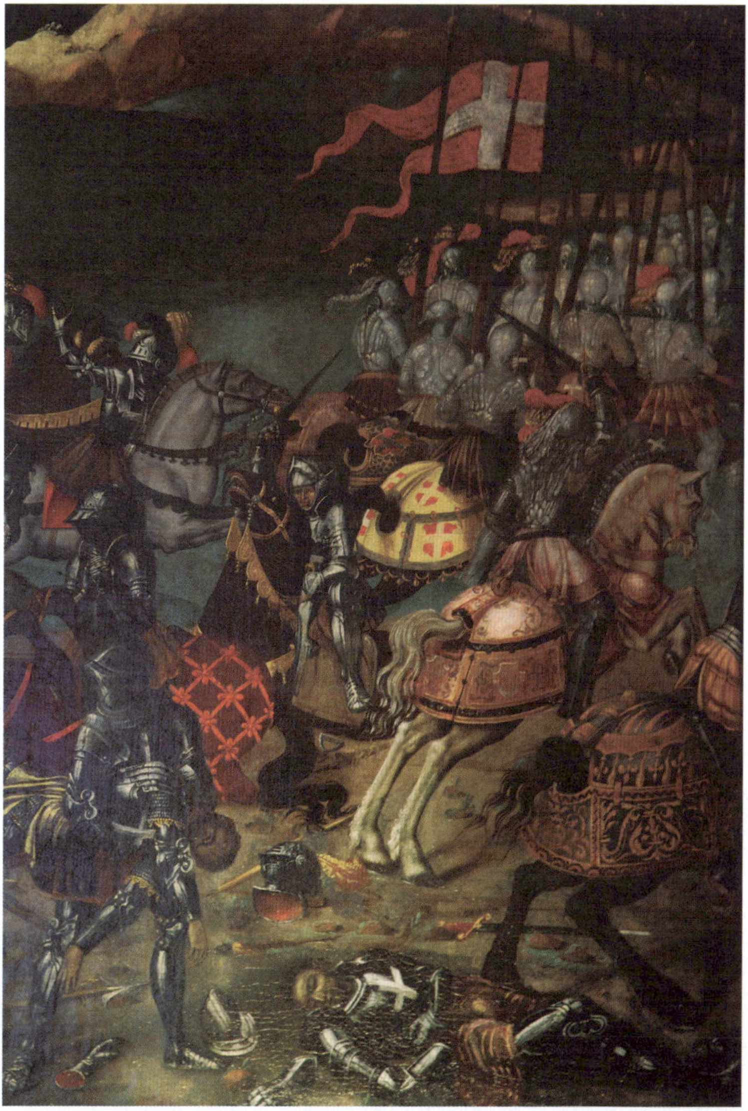

Detail from *The Battle of the Spurs, c.* 1513. The picture brutally reveals the anguish of war.

There appears to have been a centre of armour production in London before the reign of Henry VIII, but this was replaced *c.* 1515 when Henry established the royal workshops at Greenwich. The new workshop included four hammermen, three polishers and an apprentice who made armour exclusively for the king under the directorship of Martin van Royne, who was brought to England from the Netherlands by Henry. He was later replaced as master armourer by one Erasmus Kyrkenar but mention of Royne remains in the records where he is rather endearingly referred to as 'Old Martin'.

The first armour known to have been made in the royal workshop is a silvered and engraved suit to celebrate the marriage of Henry VIII and Katherine of Aragon, which can be seen today at the Tower of London. It was completed *c.* 1515, two years after the Battle of the Spurs, and is embellished with Tudor roses and the pomegranates of Aragon. A touching aspect of the decoration can be seen around the base of the tonlet (skirt) where the initials 'H and K' (for Henry and Katherine) are joined by true lover's knots and cast in copper alloy. The colour of gold, they stand out in sharp relief against the silvered background.

The process of putting on a full suit of armour usually began with the legs. The protection for the upper body and arms followed and the gauntlets and helmet were placed last. Tournament armour could be heavier than field armour because it was made for limited wear, the last pieces being added when the wearer was already in the saddle.

Contrary to countless depictions, battle armour was not heavy enough to require its wearer to be hoisted into the saddle. Most suits of armour allowed a man to mount or dismount a horse, to sit down, to run and to move his limbs without discomfort. A suit of field armour weighed around 20–25kg with the helmet weighing between 2–4kg. For comparison, the equipment of a police officer on duty today is around 20kg and an infantry soldier in the British Army must carry 20–25kg for 8 miles in two hours to pass the annual fitness test.

As mentioned previously, battle was a hard and bloody experience with horrendous wounds inflicted by the instruments of war. At the Battle of the Spurs, the traditional pole weapons known as 'bills' were employed, along with longbows, which remained a formidable weapon in the hands of experienced English archers. The design for bills had grown from agricultural tools. They comprised a cutting blade and a hook on the end of a pole in the manner of a halberd. English bills appear to have been around 6ft long. The blade end could chop and slice the victim while the hook fitted into any chinks in the enemies' armour and could dismount them, leaving them on the ground and vulnerable to the blade of the bill. Swords were also used, mostly single-handed and weighing around 1–2kg, but the two-handed sword weighed up to 4.5kg and in the hands of a skilled warrior it could cut through armour.

Seven years after Flodden Field and the Battle of the Spurs, the 28-year-old Henry was persuaded by his chief adviser, Cardinal Thomas Wolsey, that not only was war an expense that he could ill afford, it was not in keeping with the new Renaissance humanist ideals, in which a prince should make peace. For a European monarch, diplomacy was now to be preferred over battle. The Field of the Cloth of Gold in 1520 was to be an event in which the battle between the kings of England and France was a symbolic rather than physical challenge.

At the beginning of his reign, Henry VIII was hailed as the most glorious young prince in Christendom, but soon his reputation was challenged by two younger European leaders. The most powerful of Henry's rivals was Charles V, Lord of the Netherlands at 6, King of Spain at 16 and now, at just 20 years old, head of the Hapsburg dynasty and Holy Roman Emperor. Henry's second rival in what became a diplomatic triangle was Francis I, King of France. He was almost three years younger than Henry, and he ruled an expanding nation that by 1520 had a population of 12 million. The tax system of France allowed the monarch to raise taxes without government approval, whereas Henry needed to summon a parliament. France also had a standing army which Henry did not. As well as being more powerful than Henry, Francis was tall and equally magnificent. Among these three young men in their 20s, the rivalry became personal. Each made enquiries about the other as to who was the tallest (Francis?) who had the most illustrious beard (Francis?) and who could display the best calf (Henry?). Henry's trump card, however, was that he was being wooed by both sides; England might have been a minor power but she was seen as a useful ally, especially when it came to maintaining a balance of power in Europe.

In the early part of Henry's reign, new designs for armour were sparked by a better understanding of the human body and by changes in courtly fashion. The foot defences known as sabatons, for example, were no longer pointed in the fashion of a medieval shoe but wide and flat, following the pattern of court shoes seen in portraits of Henry VIII. The waist was accentuated and there was a large codpiece. The codpiece was a separate piece of armour made to protect the genitals. It was heavily padded on the inside and it remained in fashion until around 1570. It was usually only found on foot armour and, although it did offer some protection, it was more of a fashion statement taken from courtly costume and it varied in size and shape according to the choice of the wearer.

It is rare for a suit of armour to completely cover the body because the weight of the extra overlapping metal plates made it exceptionally heavy and unwieldy to move around in, but Henry had such a suit made for him to wear at the Field of the Cloth of Gold. There is no other example of armour like it in the Royal Collection armouries. It was close fitting and enhanced the young king's physique. Each plate of steel fitted flawlessly over the other which increased the weight of this unusual piece to 42.6kg, approximately twice the weight of usual foot combat armour. It gave great protection and freedom of movement to the wearer, but it would have required a youthful and physically fit body like Henry's to carry it.

In 1962, in a curious leap of history, the Royal Armouries was approached by a company called AiResearch, a manufacturer of turboprop engines and a pioneer in aerospace technology. They were one of the firms responsible for designing spacesuits for NASA (National Aeronautics and Space Administration) to be worn by astronauts. Data and photographs of Henry's armour in the Tower of London, with its overlapping steel plates, were requested and were sent by the Armouries to engineers working on the project. It was deemed helpful, and in the 1970s, NASA sent a replica Apollo suit to London to be photographed next to the armour of Henry VIII.

However, Henry's armour was never completely finished. Before the Field of the Cloth of Gold gathering, Francis I of France changed the rules of foot combat competitions. He specified that fighting would now take place over a barrier with a sword rather than in an enclosure with a poll axe. Fighting over a barrier kept the opponents further apart and so the armour could be less protective and more decorative. The new specifications required the armour to have a tonlet and a great basinet (helmet). And so, Henry abandoned the close-fitting Greenwich armour and had a second suit hurriedly made by assembling pieces already in stock. It was coloured and decorated and was finally worn by Henry at the Field of the Cloth of Gold.

The Field of the Cloth of Gold

English school, c. 1545, oil on canvas, Royal Collection Trust

By 1518 Cardinal Wolsey had formulated a non-aggression pact between these three young kings, promoting Henry not as a warrior, but as a great peacemaker. Less than a year later this treaty was in danger of falling apart, so Wolsey arranged a meeting between Henry VIII and Charles V, and then a summit between Henry and Francis. The latter became known as the Field of the Cloth of Gold, deriving its name from the sumptuousness of the materials used for the tents, pavilions and other furnishings. Henry was now almost 29 and Francis was three years younger. The diplomatic reason for the meeting was to celebrate peace but, in reality, it became a vehicle for the two young, flamboyant and ambitious monarchs to outshine each other in all manner of ways possible.

The initial challenge for Wolsey lay in finding a site acceptable to both England and France. If it was held in England, Henry would have the home advantage, while in France that benefit would have been with Francis. It was therefore decided to build the English camp at Guines, near Calais – English territory within France. The French established their base at Ardres and the language chosen for the event was French.

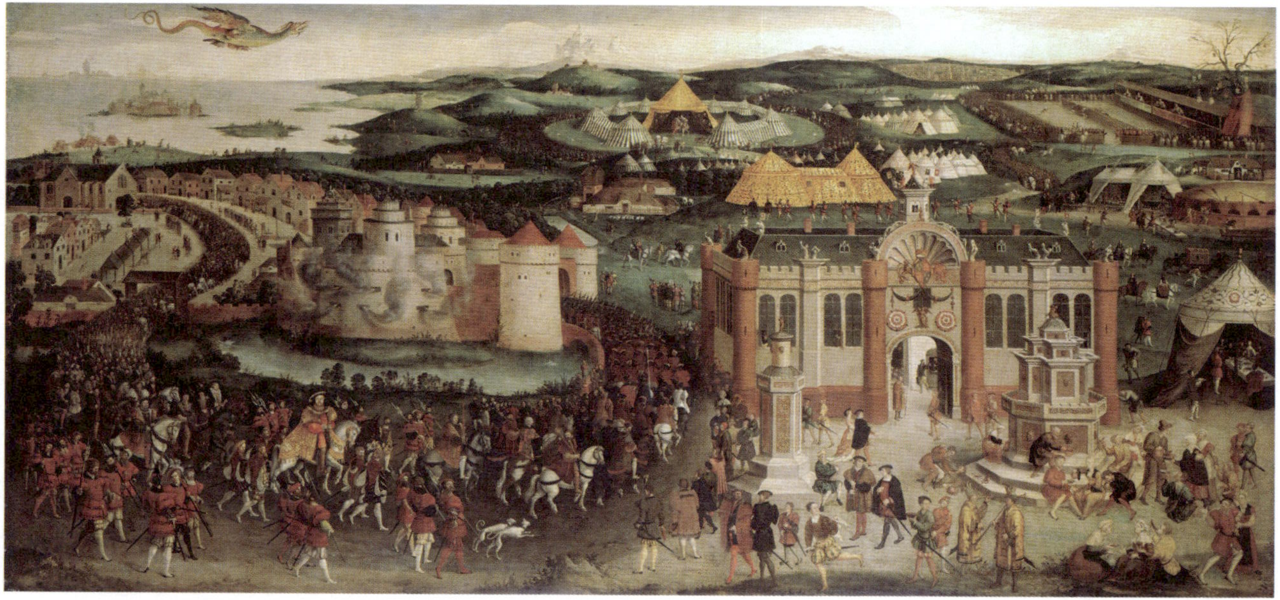

The Field of the Cloth of Gold of June 1520. This picture was painted around twenty-five years after the spectacular event.

The meeting was masterminded to the highest degree to ensure that neither of the kings would have the slightest advantage. Even the landscape was altered, so that neither Henry nor Francis would enjoy a higher ground on which to place their camp. The site of the Field of the Cloth of Gold is today in the Nord-Pas-de-Calais of France. The field in which the meeting took place is marked by a huge granite edifice stating the date and name of this event but, disappointingly, there is absolutely nothing else left to see.

The picture *The Field of the Cloth of Gold* was painted twenty years or so after the event, but the spectacle it depicts is so well chronicled that the results are likely to be reliable. We can imagine the noise, the sheer numbers of people, the transporting of horses, the beer and wine barrels, and all the provisions for a veritable army of courtiers and servants.

The two kings arrived, each with their entourage, and stayed for around two weeks in June 1520. Both were determined to be the most magnificently dressed, the best at sports, the strongest at the joust and the most charming both in dancing and in conversation. Both aspired to be true Renaissance men, and the Renaissance ideal of universal peace was in this instance to be achieved through splendour and magnificence. Each monarch was accompanied by 6,000 dukes, marquises, earls, lords, bishops, ladies, heralds, minstrels and servants who were fed, clothed and entertained to the highest standard. The French had 400 tents and the English claimed 800 'lodgings'. The English tents covered an area the size of the town of Norwich, which must surely have impressed the French.

The most imposing building in this picture is the temporary palace in the centre, where the elite of the English party were lodged. The first 8ft of the construction was built from brick; wooden struts were then inserted and canvas was rolled over them to create a huge marquee. The building was large – 100m long – and of classical design. It contained bay windows and 5,000ft of clear glass in gilded wooden frames. The canvas was decorated with heavy plaster embellishments and adorned with painted shields to enhance the appearance of substance. Inside the palace doors we can see the line of a grand staircase. It had its own chapel attended by thirty-five priests. Many of Henry and Wolsey's finest tapestries, and their best gold plate and other valuables, were taken over to France temporarily to decorate this palace. The structure was well built and during a storm, when many tents were blown away, it held fast.

When Henry entertained, it was on a grand scale. Royal Household accounts record that the fountains in front of the palace ran with more than 200,000 litres of wine – about 4 pints for everyone present. There were 66,000 litres of beer along with the equipment to brew more. The English party took all the food necessary for the trip because Henry's pride would not have allowed him to accept favours from Francis. In the fish larder alone, there were 9,100 plaice, 2,800 crayfish, three porpoises and a dolphin.

It is clear that picking up one of the terracotta jugs and helping oneself to the wine flowing from the fountains has proved tempting. On top of each fountain is a gold statue; Bacchus on the left and Cupid on the right, perhaps in anticipation of the events unfolding around them. On the steps of the fountain a brawl has broken out. A jug is broken and one of the men is aiming a punch. In the centre, to the right of the fountain steps, a man in a brown tunic and red stockings has fallen asleep on the back of the woman in front of him. The consequences of excessive alcohol consumption were the same then as now, and beside the right-hand turret of the palace a man wearing a green tunic can be seen vomiting. To the bottom right-hand corner, a male figure is being led away from the scene by a woman, her arms linked with his to support him. A closer look confirms that his heels are not touching the ground. He is waving a farewell to other figures who are returning his greeting, and it is tempting to imagine that he is letting them know that he will soon be back to carry on the party.

To the left-hand side we see the pomp and ceremony surrounding a monarch; cloth of gold abounds and the whole field would have glinted in the sun. Henry's entourage are well dressed, for keeping up appearances was essential. Many of those who accompanied him literally 'wore their estates on their backs', meaning they had mortgaged or sold parts of their estates to afford the fine clothes they are wearing. The French women were recorded as dressed in the finest Italian Renaissance fashions, which were considered by the English to be rather provocative, but it didn't take long before the English ladies were copying their French counterparts. Remarks from the Italian Ambassador hint that he was bemused by this and thought the women overly seductive.

Riding beside Henry VIII on a donkey is Cardinal Wolsey, now papal legate and representative of the Pope in England. Wolsey was recognised as an international figure of great standing. This was a man of tremendous power, intellect and eloquence, and yet he chose to ride to the event in humility, on a donkey – but a donkey adorned with gold finery.

The jousting ground can be seen in the top right-hand corner, with a tree from which painted shields hang, indicating the various jousting competitions. A knight would touch the relevant shield with his lance to confirm his wish to be included in that particular event. The importance of the joust is underlined by the fact that a steel mill was floated over the channel from Greenwich to produce steel for the feats of arms during this two-week event. Jousting took place every day except Sunday, when Henry went to dinner with Queen Claude of France and Francis dined with Katherine, Queen of England. Each king was expected to arrive at the other's camp at exactly the same time, and so at the sound of a trumpet both would leave their respective camps. They rode across the countryside and raced towards each other in mock combat, only turning their horses away at the last second. This was horseplay between two young, physically able men in their 20s who just happened to be kings.

A religious mass closed this grand meeting with Cardinal Wolsey proclaiming a general indulgence, forgiving the sins of everyone present. The English then released a canvas and wooden kite of a mythical beast, attached to a carriage and pulled through the air. The shape of the creature could be interpreted as both the salamander emblem of Francis I and the Welsh dragon for Henry VIII. Fireworks were lit inside the kite, making its eyes glow like fire, and smoke hissed from its mouth. And so the Field of the Cloth of Gold passed into history as one of the most spectacular events in Tudor diplomacy. However, the peace hoped for by Wolsey, when masterminding the meeting, lasted for less than two years. In the Italian War of 1521–26, Henry VIII joined forces with the Holy Roman Emperor, Charles V, against the armies of Francis I. As Erasmus said, 'Kings and Princes will never agree.'

3

PAINTED JEWELS: MINIATURES AND STAINED GLASS

PAINTING IN LITTLE ... WHICH EXCELLETH ALL OTHER PAINTING WHATSOEVER.

NICHOLAS HILLIARD
THE ARTE OF LIMNING, 1590

MINIATURE PAINTINGS

IN DECEMBER 1526, England and France were once again on cordial terms and Henry VIII received a gift of two gold lockets from the sister of King Francis. One contained a small portrait of 'Francis very naturally painted' and in the other was a tiny picture of the Dauphin and his brother, Henry. The following year, in fine diplomatic form, Henry returned a gift to Francis of two miniature portraits. One was of himself and the other was of his daughter Mary, his child by Katherine of Aragon, to whom he had been married for seventeen years. It was at this time in England that the portrait miniature – or 'seeing in little' – emerged as a distinctly separate art form from conventional portrait painting.

By the mid 1520s, the Flemish Horenbout family had arrived in England: Gerard Horenbout and his children Lucas and Suzanna. Both offspring were illuminators and most likely received their instruction in their father's workshop. Their work represents the first important pre-Holbein series of portraits in the reign of Henry VIII.

Lucas learned his trade in Ghent with his father, who was court artist to Margaret of Austria (Regent of the Netherlands). He was employed by Henry VIII from *c.* 1525 and remained in the king's service until his death *c.* 1544. From 1534, he was appointed King's Painter on an annual salary of £33 6*s* (over 10 per cent more than Holbein received).

His sister, Suzanna, was also a gifted artist. The German painter and printmaker Albrecht Durer was impressed with her skill and acquired a miniature by her, for which he paid 1 florin. He noted that, 'It is very wonderful that a woman can do so much,' a remark that deserves no further comment!

In the Tudor age, tiny paintings like this were not called 'miniatures' but 'limnings,'a term used in the production of manuscripts. The history of portrait miniatures began with artists trained to illustrate documents and handwritten books.

The concept of a small portrait – or limning – derived from images that emerged in antiquity on coins, medals or cameo jewellery. By the sixteenth century, the miniature portrait reproduced images found in sacred illuminated manuscripts. These rich and expensive religious books were created by hand for private chapels or as gifts to religious institutions, and they often incorporated a tiny, hand-painted picture of the patron. Once the technology was available to produce books in printed form the limner was effectively made redundant, apart from small numbers of commissions to embellish books. Many of these specialists in miniature portraits then set up their own independent workshops promoting portrait miniatures as a stand-alone form of art. In its conception and reproduction, the miniature painting is a totally different genre to a standard portrait and the two cannot be directly compared. The style and technique of painting in miniature developed in the Flemish workshops of Bruges and Ghent before finding popularity in France and England.

Henry VIII

Lucas Horenbout, 1525, Fitzwilliam Museum, Cambridge

The earliest known English miniature is of a beardless Henry VIII produced around 1525 by Lucas Horenbout. The picture is inscribed: 'H.R./VIII' and 'ANO.ETATIS/XXXVO'. This suggests that Henry VIII was in his 35th year. There is mention of a payment to Horenbout in the autumn of 1525 and the attribution is also made because he was the only artist in England at the time capable of painting the work.

To colour Henry's face, Horenbout has built up the image with short brushstrokes on a base of opaque carnation ground which gives it the pinkish colour, still visible. The border decoration is rare for a miniature portrait. It conforms to that seen on manuscripts from the Ghent and Bruges school, where Horenbout trained. Particularly reminiscent of manuscript design are the flying angels on the frame, holding censers and painted in gold. The entwined initials 'H and K' at the upper and lower frame refer to Henry VIII and Katherine of Aragon. The image is tiny – only 53mm x 48mm. The Society of Miniature Painters demands a maximum frame size of 151mm x 113mm and the primary requisite of any miniature portrait remains exquisite detail.

There is a group of seven miniatures of Henry VIII by Horenbout in the Royal Collection but only one of them shows Henry clean-shaven. The king would frequently grow a beard and then remove it after a short time. In August 1519, in a manly challenge to Francis I, he suggested that neither king shave until they met at the Field of the Cloth of Gold. It would be a way for both monarchs to show commitment to their meeting and – to add competition – whoever displayed the most illustrious beard would be the victor. Of course, Henry was a red-haired Englishman and Francis a dark-haired Frenchman, so the latter was more likely to win. Perhaps having failed to grow the magnificent beard he had expected, it was a clean-shaven Henry that greeted his rival, having removed his beard by November 1519.

On being asked for an explanation of Henry's appearance, Thomas Boleyn, English Ambassador to France, commented, 'As I suppose, it hath been by the Queen's desire; for ... I have heard hereafore time known when the King's grace hath worn long his beard, that the Queen hath daily made him great instance, and desired him put it off for her sake.'

Miniature portraits were produced in watercolour on animal skin, usually calf, that was stretched and primed until it was almost translucent. It was produced using the same technique as that employed in books and manuscripts, but the vellum for portraits was generally thinner. The vellum was then attached to a support with

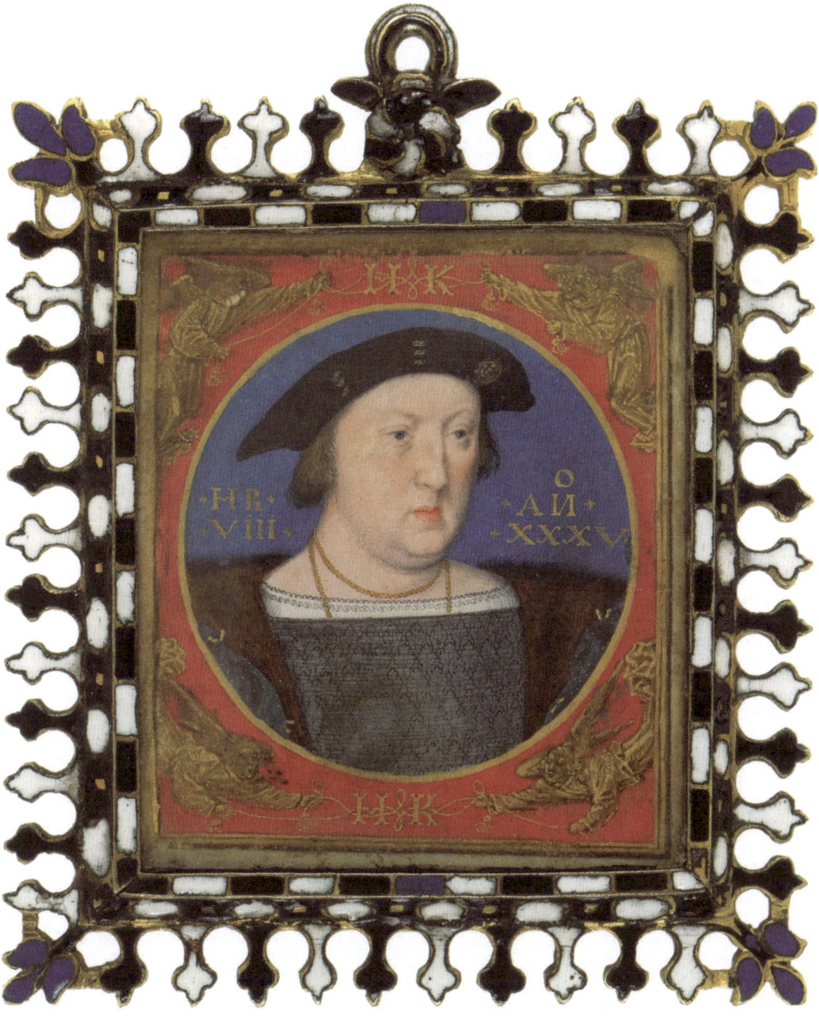

Lucas Horenbout's depiction of Henry VIII is the earliest example of a portrait miniature in England.

starch paste. Playing cards were manufactured from sheets of paper glued together and as such, they provided an ideal and commonly used backing for portrait miniatures. The face of the playing card can sometimes remain visible, leading to descriptions such as that of the Horenbout miniature of Henry VIII in the Royal Collection: 'vellum laid on playing card (the ace of diamonds)'. To smooth the vellum and merge it with the support, it was rubbed with an animal tooth – usually one belonging to a large dog – set into a wooden handle.

Pigments were ground to a fine powder and mixed with water in a mussel shell, the ideal disposable container for small quantities of paint. If an opaque result was required, gum Arabic or glair manufactured from egg white was added. The fine brushes necessary to paint such minute detail were usually fabricated from squirrel hair, which was set into a wooden handle. It was advised that artists should wear silk while painting and not even breathe over their works for fear of damaging then with fibres or spittle.

A portrait miniature was intended to be held in the hand and admired, and it could be decorated by wealthy individuals, to the point where the setting was more valuable than the portrait. The opulence of the painted jewels was achieved by first painting their outline with dark ochre and then embellishing them with real gold or silver that was burnished until it shone by using a tiny tooth – often from a stoat or similar – on the end of a wooden handle. This technique was intended to give the viewer the impression that the small painting shining in their hands was rich in gemstones – and as valuable. Jewels were not just valued for their monetary worth, but on a mystical and symbolic level as well. There was a belief that certain precious stones possessed spiritual qualities that would fend off evil, drive away fear and overcome sorrow. The small size of these miniature portraits lent them to being worn close to the body to increase their potency. Such was the skill in painting miniatures that, regardless of their small size, they retained their impact. They have all the qualities of fine art but on a reduced scale.

Both Horenbout and Holbein used a circular format for their portrait miniatures; both fixed the vellum to a playing card and both applied the same dense blue background. However, the similarities end there because these two men came from different artistic backgrounds. Horenbout, who trained as a painter of illuminated manuscripts, built up the face in flat, even strokes that followed the edge of the frame, whereas Holbein was accustomed to painting in oils, and his brushstrokes followed the contours of the sitter's body as would have happened in larger oil paintings. Holbein was a left-handed painter and he would have set up the painting slope (a small portable desk originating from the medieval lectern used for producing illuminated manuscripts) in the opposite direction to Horenbout so as not to block out the light with his hand.

Horenbout is credited with teaching Hans Holbein the art of limning, and Holbein painted a round miniature of Erasmus in 1531–32. He in turn inspired the Elizabethan miniaturist Nicholas Hilliard, the first native-born master of the form, who said, 'Holbein's manner of limning I have ever imitated and hold it for the best.'

Portrait miniatures saw a substantial growth in popularity throughout the Tudor period. Twenty-two miniatures have been attributed to Horenbout from the time of his employment at the court of Henry VIII. They were easily portable and were sought out by soldiers, sailors and merchants who desired an image of their loved one that could be held close to them as they travelled the world. Alternatively, they could be worn intimately next to the body of a wife or mistress left behind in England. Their tiny size meant that the patron could decide who saw them, unlike an oil painting on the wall in open view. Miniatures were extremely sought after in the case of illicit relationships, as it was easy to conceal the image from prying eyes. Only three people needed to know the identity of the sitter: the artist, the patron and the subject themselves. In other words, these diminutive pictures were used like photographs or social media today. With the advent of photography in the mid-nineteenth century, the art of the miniature portrait declined, and artists were forced to find additional employment in colour-tinting black and white photographs.

It was Henry VIII who initiated the fashion for portrait miniatures in England, and our present queen, Her Majesty Queen Elizabeth II, has expanded the collection. The Royal Collection today contains over 3,000 of these tiny paintings, one of the most comprehensive groupings of portrait miniatures in the world.

STAINED GLASS

Henry VIII spent lavishly on the decoration of his palaces, with badges, mottoes and heraldry forming an outer layer of propaganda upon the shell of each building. Stained glass was an essential part of this magnificence, with every jewel-like symbol proclaiming the king's power, at a time when glass windows could only be seen in churches and very wealthy homes. Most visible were the Tudor rose, the logo of the Tudor dynasty, the Beaufort portcullis, the royal coat of arms, and the fleur-de-lys, marking Henry's claim to the throne of France. These beautiful images in glass could also tell stories and disperse moral guidance, allowing Henry to identify himself with great historic, religious and mythological figures. Just as stained glass filled the viewer with wonder on entering the house of God, here one might feel the same sense of awe on entering the house of the king. Hardly any decorated glass survives from Henry's palaces, but it is believed that figural glass was only used in the chapels, to depict saints and angels, while heraldic glass was prolific throughout the rest of the buildings.

To the average Tudor, stained glass-making was aligned to alchemy; it was a mysterious process that turned base materials into imitation gems. The insertion of coloured-glass windows converted a formerly dark room into a box of jewels. The names for the colours of glass were those of precious stones: ruby, sapphire, emerald, amethyst. When the sun shone, the panels glowed like precious stones and cast flickering colours over the surface of all the walls. So impressive was it that for special occasions, glaziers would hire out portable panels to those unable to afford a permanent installation.

In the Middle Ages, gorgeous pieces of coloured glass set into high gothic pillars transformed church interiors and led congregations to view the light of God. Aware of its propaganda potential, Henry VIII had more stained glass installed into his palaces than his father had done, and appreciated the status it awarded him among European leaders.

Tudor homes able to afford glass windows typically installed them as small diamond-shape panes called 'quarries' (from the French *carrées*, meaning square), held together in a lattice pattern with strips of lead. For those without the finances to purchase window glass in any form, horn, oiled linen, parchment or even paper was employed to protect a home from the elements.

The glass-making process had changed little since the Romans first created it. Making a stained-glass panel bears many similarities to producing a Tudor tapestry. The glazier drew a set of small sketches of each design for the patron's approval. Any changes were ideally made at this stage. Once the composition was agreed, the glazier and the patron each kept a copy of the sketch to resolve potential disagreements after fabrication.

The glazier enlarges the design onto a piece of paper the same size and shape as the window. This was the pattern, known as a 'cartoon' – the same term used for templates of tapestries and wall paintings. Cut-lines were marked on the paper pattern, indicating where and in what shape the glass pieces were to be cut. Colours were discussed and sheets of the required panes were placed on order. The glassmakers supplied the materials but did not usually make the windows as that was the job of the glazier.

The highest quality glass was produced in Normandy. These fragile sheets would be wrapped in straw, packed in wooden crates and transported by boat. Once all the glass arrived, the glazier laid them on the pattern and cut each piece into shape using the cut-lines as a template. It was a challenging process during which fragments were easily broken. On completion, all the pieces were laid out on the pattern and any that required extra detail – for example a face, the folds of a garment or a motto – were painted or stained and then refired in the kiln to make them permanent. The completed design was positioned in the window piece by piece, supported by lead strips.

Henry VIII's main glazier was Galyon Hone, who described himself as 'native of Holland and a subject of the Emperor'. He trained in Antwerp and settled in England in

1510. Hone lived in a house with a garden in Southwark, a district that lay just outside the jurisdiction of the City of London. Foreign craftsmen could work in this area without being members of the city guilds and, as a consequence, it was an area populated mainly by immigrant workers. It had a bad reputation, being notorious for 'loose women, scavengers and scroungers and unclean trades'. In 1523, an Act of law extended the authority of the City of London by 2 miles, suddenly bringing Southwark within the control of the guilds and removing the former privileges of its residents. Affected by the restrictions imposed on him and possibly in search of more work space, Hone leased a dwelling in the precincts of St Thomas's hospital. Although still in Southwark, it was situated on land owned by the church and was therefore classed as a 'Liberty'. This meant that Hone was not forced to abide by the regulations of the Worshipful Company of Glaziers and could challenge their monopoly, which he appears to have done. Hone was arrested and imprisoned in 1538 for working outside the Liberty. He was released following the intervention of powerful members of the Tudor court. These were men who had employed Hone to reproduce the decorative schemes he had completed for the king in their own palatial properties. The area has changed somewhat today, but the Glaziers Company headquarters remains in Southwark.

One of Galyon Hone's first commissions for King Henry VIII was at Bridewell Palace, a former home of Cardinal Wolsey that became Henry's base in London after a fire at Westminster Palace in 1512. Henry VIII spent £20,000 on this house near Blackfriars. It was leased, in 1531, to the French ambassador Jean de Dinteville and would become the setting for Hans Holbein's famous painting *The Ambassadors*.

Hone also repaired all the old windows for Henry at Hunsdon Manor, Hertfordshire and he received 12 pennies per badge at Oaklands and Eltham palaces for creating roses, portcullises and hawthorns – popular emblems representing Tudor ancestry. Given Cardinal Wolsey's animosity toward Anne Boleyn, he may have been feeling the need to appease the king when he commissioned Hone to install the arms of the Boleyn family into various windows.

Henry VIII demolished Wolsey's Great Hall at Hampton Court and from 1532 built a larger replacement filled with beautiful stained-glass windows. Hone made thirty coats of arms and forty-six badges. At each end of the hall were two great arms with four beasts on them. In addition, he produced thirty-six new windows for Henry's watching chamber, or guard room. The purpose of the entire room was to impress the visitor, for this was the king's entrance hall. The ceiling was remarkably high, at 60ft, and its ultimate glory was the windows, installed on a scale to make the individual feel insignificant. When Henry VIII stood on the dais (raised platform) at the end of his great hall, lit by the light streaming through his heraldic glass, he would have seemed an awe-inspiring figure.

The most personal and intriguing of Galyon Hone's work for Henry VIII was during Henry's romance with Anne Boleyn. He was commissioned to place glass into fourty-eight openings in 'the mount in the garden', a hill at the end of the chief pleasure garden overlooking the river, where the lovers used to meet. The poet John Skelton described Hampton Court as, 'with turrets and towers, with halls and bowers, stretching to the stars, with glass windows and bars'.

Henry's habitual remarrying kept Galyon Hone and other craftsmen busy for many years, as they replaced the badges of each queen throughout his numerous homes. At Greenwich Palace, Hone replaced Katherine of Aragon's crests with those of Anne Boleyn and, following Anne's fall and execution in 1536, her arms were in turn superseded by those of Jane Seymour.

In the Great Hall at Hampton Court, Hone produced badges that were 'set into the garlands of the former Queen' in order to save time and money. By removing the spots from Anne's leopard, Hone transformed it into Jane's panther. With similar adjustments to Anne's falcon badge, it metamorphosed into the phoenix of Jane Seymour. Anne's stained-glass figure in the chapel was removed less than a year after its completion. At Greenwich Palace, Hone similarly supplanted the stained glass of each of Henry's successive wives.

Window of Henry VIII and Katherine of Aragon

St Margaret's Church, Westminster

All of Henry's queens had their arms produced in stained glass and at least one of each design still exists, although not *in situ*. From Henry's buildings, a single stained-glass window survives. Although not produced for its present home, there is a panel in St Margaret's Church, Westminster, that depicts a crucifixion with King Henry, Katherine of Aragon and their patron saints immortalised together in stained glass. It was made in the Netherlands *c.* 1526. Unfortunately, by the time this beautiful window was completed, Henry only had eyes for Anne Boleyn.

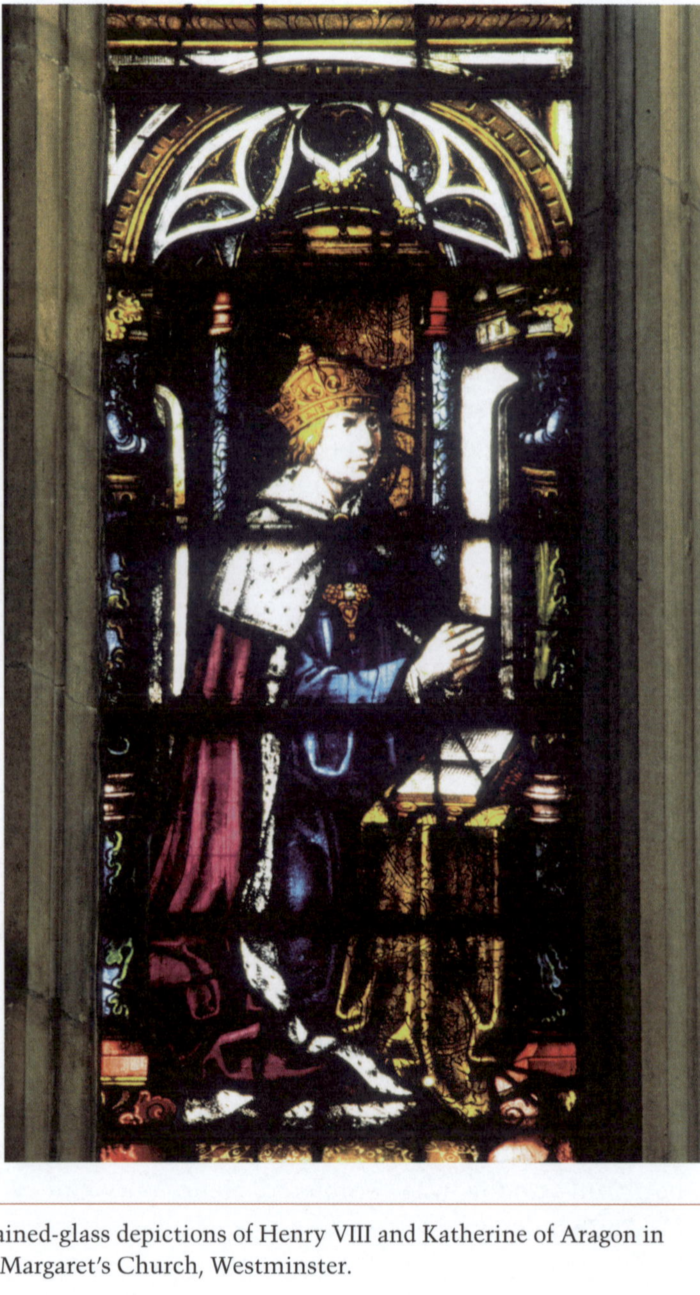

Stained-glass depictions of Henry VIII and Katherine of Aragon in St Margaret's Church, Westminster.

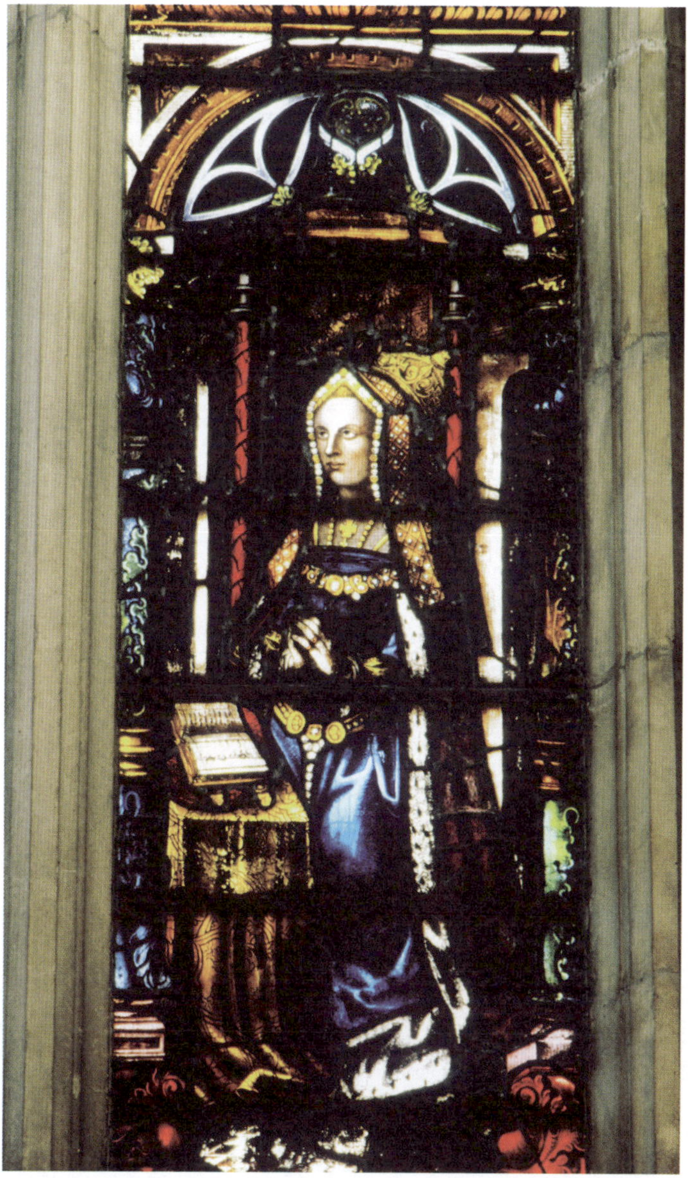

4

THE BREAK FROM ROME: STONING THE POPE

PRESUMPTUOUS POPES WERE FORCED TO YIELD BEFORE HIM ... AND TRUE RELIGION WAS ESTABLISHED.

WHITEHALL MURAL

FOR THE FIRST HALF of his reign, the most striking aspect of Henry VIII's attitude to Rome was his conformity. He enjoyed a mutually beneficial relationship with several Popes, who blessed all his enterprises. Religion was an integral part of the king's daily life and he had a genuine interest in theology, which he enjoyed debating. In 1521 the Pope awarded Henry the title 'Defender of the Faith' for his support of the papacy and condemnation of Martin Luther, the German monk whose teachings inspired the Protestant Reformation. The title is still carried by the English monarch to this day.

To the end of his days Henry would be conservative in his religious beliefs, deploring Lutheran heresies.

He believed in Purgatory and clerical celibacy, maintained Latin rituals and endorsed painted images. But Henry's break with Rome, his establishment of the Royal Supremacy, the English Bible and the dissolution of the monasteries would arguably be the most far-reaching events of his reign, and his most lasting legacy.

THE GREAT MATTER

The 'King's Great Matter' was a phrase used at the time to describe political and religious questioning in England, ignited by Henry VIII's desire for an annulment of his marriage to Katherine of Aragon. (An annulment of a marriage returns the couple to their original unmarried state as though the union had never taken place, whereas a divorce cancels their married status from the present time.)

By 1527, Katherine of Aragon was 42 years old, with one surviving child: her daughter Mary. It was clear the queen would not produce a male heir, and Henry's longing for a son was much more than a personal whim. England had been torn apart by the Wars of the Roses of the previous century. Were he to die without a strong successor, civil war might be renewed.

The king's passion for Anne Boleyn, the charismatic young lady he wished to marry, combined with the political necessity of producing a male heir, made Henry determined to find a solution. Ever religious, Henry now came to the conclusion that his marriage to Katherine was unlawful in the sight of God because she had previously been married to his brother, Arthur.

According to Henry, the union contravened Divine Law and he quoted Leviticus 20:21, which forbids a man to marry his brother's widow. Furthermore, he claimed that they were without a male heir as a penalty for living in mortal sin, even though a dispensation from the Pope in the first instance had allowed him to marry Katherine. In his enthusiasm to marry Katherine in 1509 the young Henry had overlooked this impediment; now his conscience was greatly troubled.

Pope Clement VII faced a problem; if he granted the annulment it was tantamount to announcing that his predecessor, Pope Julius II, had made an error by granting a dispensation in the first place. For more than two decades there had been no questioning of the validity of the dispensation and Katherine was determined not to be set aside. The battle lines were thus drawn up and years of negotiations followed, with the king becoming increasingly frustrated.

Anne Boleyn and her family were attracted to Reformist doctrine and this had a significant impact on Henry. Anne was in a unique position to influence the king by bringing new theological ideas and Lutheran writings to his attention. She may have shown Henry *The Obedience of a Christian Man*, a work by the English Protestant William Tyndale. The book denounced the evils of the Catholic Church and suggested that the king of a country was the head of that country's Church, rather than the Pope. Henry concluded it was 'the book for me and all kings to read'. Whether from ambition or genuine religious belief, Anne thus played a major part in pushing Henry into asserting his headship of the English Church.

Sensing danger, Cardinal Wolsey instructed all English agents in Rome that if the Pope did not issue the annulment Henry sought, the consequences would be extreme. If Henry could not obtain justice from Clement VII, he would be compelled to seek it by some other means. The church lawyer, Stephen Gardiner, who was serving as one of Henry's diplomats, explicitly told the Pope that 'the King's highness would do it without him'.

But Clement was in a politically impossible situation: the armies of Katherine's nephew Charles V had sacked Rome in 1527. Charles had effectively placed the Pope under arrest and applied intense pressure on him to resist the annulment of his aunt's marriage. Wolsey failed to obtain the annulment and he made an enemy of the now powerful Boleyn family. In 1529 he lost the king's favour for good. Deprived of his great offices and possessions, he was eventually arrested for treason. Had he not died at Leicester Abbey in 1530, Wolsey would almost certainly have been executed by Henry VIII. The continuing task of obtaining the annulment then fell to Wolsey's successor as Chancellor, Sir Thomas More, a devout Catholic who would never deny the authority of the Pope.

In January 1533, Henry married Anne, who was pregnant, and events now began to move at a quick pace. In May, the new Archbishop of Canterbury, Thomas Cranmer, sat in judgement at a special court convened to rule on the validity of the king's first marriage. Thomas Cranmer had been working on Henry's annulment for some time and would go on to become a leading figure in the English Reformation. He declared the marriage of Henry and Katherine null and void and the marriage of Henry and Anne to be good and valid. Katherine was formally stripped of her title as queen and Anne was subsequently crowned Queen Consort on 1 June 1533 in a magnificent ceremony at Westminster Abbey.

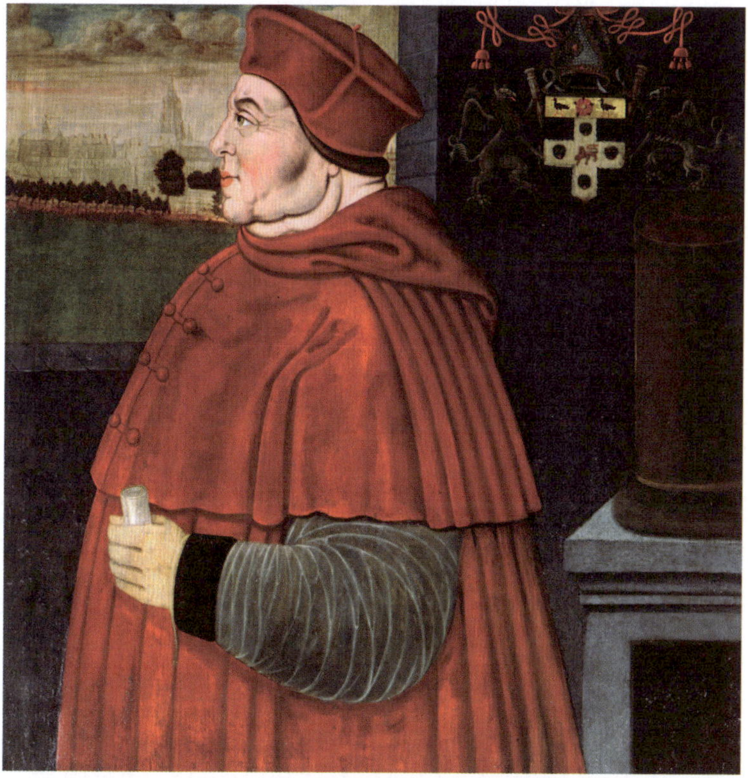

Cardinal Wolsey was an efficient administrator, but his inability to arrange an annulment for Henry led to his downfall.

BREAK FROM ROME

The Pope reacted by excommunicating both Henry and Thomas Cranmer before declaring Katherine the rightful Queen of England and ordering Henry to return to her. Henry then abandoned Rome and rejected the traditional relationship between king and Pope forever. The first Act of Supremacy, passed by the English parliament in November 1534, made the king the 'Only Head of the Church of England on Earth so far as the Law of God allows'. The whole concept of medieval kingship was overthrown by this Reformation Parliament, which now granted Henry far greater powers than any English king had ever wielded. Parliamentary Acts of 1529–39 created a radically different kingship in England, with the clergy forced to accept his authority and the king owing submission to no one but God.

Once he had established himself as Supreme Head of the Church of England, adherence to the new Church was equated with loyalty to the king. Those who did not, or could not, subscribe to the new order were to be regarded as traitors who owed their allegiance to a foreign Pope and not to the King of England. This was confirmed by the Oath of Succession, to be sworn by all government officials, recognising Anne as the lawful queen and her children as legitimate heirs to the throne. The 1534 Treasons Act made rejection of this oath punishable by death. Sir Thomas More was executed under this Act, along with John Fisher, Bishop of Rochester. In May 1535, the newly elected Pope Paul III had created Fisher Cardinal Priest of San Vitale, apparently in the hope of inducing Henry to ease Fisher's treatment. The effect was precisely the reverse: Henry forbade the cardinal's hat to be brought into England, declaring that he would send the head to Rome instead.

In the same year, the king ordered his Principal Secretary, Thomas Cromwell, to produce a report – the *Valor Ecclesiasticus* (church valuation) – to assess the wealth of the monasteries, abbeys and nunneries where more than 10,000 monks and nuns were living. While the king was not opposed to religious houses on theological grounds, there was concern over the loyalty of the monastic orders, which were international in character and resistant to the Royal Supremacy. The monasteries were a reminder of the power of the Catholic Church.

The Crown was also in financial difficulty, and the wealth of the Church made confiscation of Church property both tempting and feasible. There were more than 800 religious houses in England and Wales, which owned more than a quarter of the total land, and Henry considered that the income the Pope had previously received from the monasteries of England and Wales should now flow directly to the Crown. Cromwell also realised that he could bind the gentry and nobility to Royal Supremacy by selling them Church lands at favourable prices.

The investigation was carried out by commissioners, who were mostly local gentry. Their concern was for the monetary value of the properties, but with it came evidence of scandal and corruption. It was claimed that monks and nuns lived in excess luxury and often used fraudulent relics to encourage visiting pilgrims, or leased false tokens said to have healing powers. The damning reports contained in the *Valor Ecclesiasticus* led in 1536 to the first Act of Suppression, in which monasteries with an income of less than £200 a year were closed and their possessions taken by the Crown.

DISSOLUTION AND UNREST

Not everyone in Catholic England accepted Henry's break from Rome and there was particular unrest in the north of England. The most serious internal crisis of the reign was an uprising in the northern counties known as the Pilgrimage of Grace. It was a direct response to Henry VIII's Reformation legislation and it began at Louth in Lincolnshire in October 1536 before spreading to Yorkshire a few weeks later. Religion was of fundamental importance at all ranks of society, and tens of thousands of Englishmen were prepared to rise in protest against the king's policies. The lawyer Robert Aske became an effective leader of an army of troops and the sheer numbers of rebels involved meant the threat to the throne was grave. Thomas Howard, Duke of Norfolk and uncle of Anne Boleyn, was despatched by Henry to contain the revolt. Aske and the rebels were offered a full pardon, along with a vague promise that England would return to papal obedience and that a parliament free from royal influence would be considered. Aske naively accepted Norfolk's promises on behalf of the king and dispersed the rebel army. But Henry broke his word; martial law was declared and rebel leaders were put on trial. Several hundred rebels, including Aske, were executed.

The following year Cromwell led the dissolution of the remaining religious houses, and by 1540 all the monasteries had been closed. The last to be dissolved was Waltham Abbey in March 1540. Henry VIII gleaned the wealth of the monasteries and allowed prominent families to purchase monastic lands in return for their political support. Meanwhile the abandoned monastery buildings slowly crumbled through want of maintenance, changing the landscape of England and Wales forever.

HENRY'S RELIGION

Henry VIII portrayed himself as the religious leader who banished the vice-ridden Catholic Church from England and restored the truth of the Bible. He saw himself as King David, the Old Testament ruler who had slain the Goliath of papal corruption. But Henry also remained conservative in his religion. He continued to believe in transubstantiation (the belief that at consecration the eucharist elements become the body and blood of Christ), purgatory and clerical celibacy, and to the end of his days maintained Latin rituals. His religion was confusing to his contemporaries, who were forced to tread a careful path; he burned as heretics those who were too evangelical, and executed as traitors those loyal to the papacy. Even Henry's sixth wife, Katherine Parr, misjudged the king's stance on religion. In 1546, she came under suspicion for her reformist views, and a Catholic faction at court tried to move against her. She was about to be arrested for heresy but was forewarned (possibly with Henry's connivance) and managed a last-minute reconciliation with her husband. Throwing herself on Henry's mercy, she pleaded that she had debated with him on theology, only to learn from him and to distract him from the pain in his legs. The following day, when the Lord Chancellor arrived with soldiers to arrest the queen in Henry's presence, the king chased them away.

We can find a demonstration of Henry's religious beliefs on the frontispiece of the Great Bible of 1539 – the first authorised English translation to be read aloud in the Church of England. The illustrated page shows a semi-divine, enthroned Henry VIII at the top of the page, with a tiny image of God squeezed in above him. The king is receiving the Word of God and bestowing it upon his bishops, who in turn deliver it to the priests and the social orders. Finally, the common people hear the Word and declare, throughout the land '*Vivat Rex* [long live the king]!'

Leading his people towards 'true religion' was now incumbent in the role of the king. The inscription on the Whitehall Mural (see chapter six) makes clear that Henry has come to see the break from Rome as his greatest achievement. He claims superiority over his father, Henry VII, because he is 'born to a greater destiny… presumptuous popes were forced to yield before him … and true religion was established'.

The Great Bible was distributed to every church in England, with King Henry's role emphasised as the source of religious and secular power. In this way the new image of the king was disseminated, in a planned act of mass propaganda that makes Henry's position clear. Matters of religion would be the responsibility of the sovereign, who would be regarded as God's deputy on earth. King Henry VIII had not only rejected the Pope but taken his place.

A Protestant Allegory

Girolamo da Treviso, 1538–44, oil on panel, Royal Collection Trust

A Protestant Allegory, painted around 1538–44 by Girolamo da Treviso, powerfully endorses Henry's claim that corruption in the Catholic Church lies behind his decision to break with the Pope.

After the break with Rome, colourful, gilded, and much-loved 'Popish' images of the Virgin Mary and the Saints started to be replaced with art that depicted moral stories and narrative scenes from the Bible. Small engravings

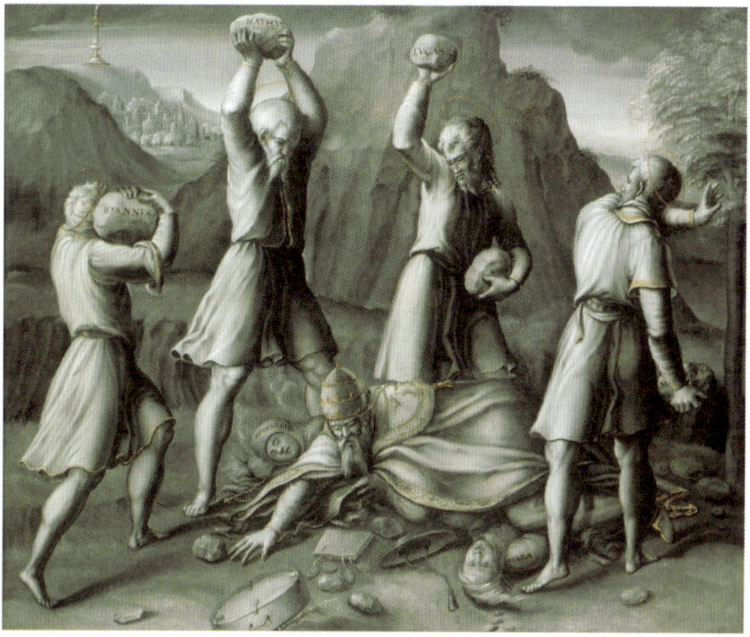

This painting is mentioned in an inventory of Henry's goods in 1547.

and prints became more popular, some of the colour in churches was lost and there was a general movement away from devotional imagery.

Grisaille, deriving from the French word *gris*, is a technique in which the image is entirely painted from different shades of grey. During the Renaissance period, it was used principally to imitate sculpture, but the modest grey effect in this picture mimics a print or an engraving. There are no rich colours to associate it with Catholic art, the only embellishments are touches of fine gold. Richness was needed as the image was intended for the king, but the magnificence of the gold was clearly for the pleasure of a monarch and not for the glory of God.

The Pope is sprawled face down on the ground, his nose next to a purse of money, suggesting corruption. Perhaps surprisingly, it is not a likeness of Henry's adversary, Pope Clement VII, who had died in September 1534, reportedly from eating poisonous mushrooms, but more closely resembles Julius II who was known as the 'warrior pope' through his use of warfare to regain and maintain control of the Papal states. After Henry's older brother Arthur died, it was Julius II who had issued the dispensation in the first instance, allowing Henry to marry his brother's widow Katherine of Aragon.

Four Evangelists are bracing themselves to cast heavy boulders. Each rock is engraved with the name of the holder, with Luke holding two stones. The Evangelists are bigger, taller and broader by far than the Pope, allowing them to dominate the scene, and they are looking down on him. Matthew has his chin hard down onto his chest; his calf muscles are strained and his tunic sways as he aims the boulder at the head of the Pope. The pose of Matthew resembles a figure in *The Stoning of Saint Stephen*, c. 1522, by Giulio Romano, whom

Girolamo da Treviso may have worked with in Italy, and the composition bears a striking resemblance to three woodcuts illustrating scenes of stoning in the Coverdale Bible of 1535, the first to be translated into English.

A Cardinal's hat rolls in the dust and a papal bull lies behind it. The papal bull is a charter issued by the Pope and it is named after the lead seals known as 'bulla' that are applied at the end of the document to authenticate it. Four bulla are splayed out in the dirt, indicating four [apal documents. The red hat was instigated by Pope Innocent IV in 1244 and awarded to a Cardinal as a privilege. Thomas Wolsey, advisor to Henry VIII, was appointed a Cardinal in 1515 and permitted to wear the Cardinal's hat, which became part of his personal coat of arms. One of the charges levelled against Wolsey in 1529 included a reference to the red hat:

> Also the said lord cardinal, of his further pompous and presumptuous mind, hath enterprised to join and imprint the cardinal's hat under your arms in your coin of groats, made at your city of York, which like deed hath not yet been seen to have been done by any subject within your realm before this time.

Following Wolsey's death at Leicester Abbey in 1530, his hat was presented to Christ Church, Oxford. Cardinal Wolsey's hat rests today in the upper library of the college he founded in 1525.

Two women are pictured, representing 'Greed' and 'Hypocrisy'. The word 'hypocrisy' derives from the ancient Greek meaning 'play-acting'. It is defined as the false appearance of virtue or goodness that conceals true character, particularly regarding religion. In the painting, the female personification is 'cloaked in hypocrisy'.

'Greed' probably pertains to the hoarding and accumulation of wealth in the Catholic Church, but it is also aligned with gluttony and one of the seven deadly sins. An extinguished candle alludes to the snuffing out of the doctrine of Rome. The cooking pan is a domestic item perhaps referring to the internal politics from which this situation emanated. Storm clouds are gathering. A lighted candle to the top left indicates hope. It suggests that the true light of religion now comes from the Gospels and from Jerusalem, the exotic town of cupolas and towers that is depicted beneath the candle.

THE ARTIST

Looking at the materials used to produce a painting can reveal an enormous amount about the work itself. Although this image is the work of an Italian artist, the evidence suggests it was produced in England. Before 1540 all portraits produced in England were painted on wooden panel, which remained the most popular medium for paintings until the end of the century. Oak from trees growing around the Hanseatic ports on the Baltic was used not just in England but in the Netherlands, parts of France and Northern Germany. Southern Germany was more likely to use lime or beech. Italy made good use of their local poplar trees and in the Veneto, panels were made from soft woods like pine or larch. Walnut or fruit wood like cherry were generally used in furniture but they were sometimes seen in painted panels on doors, chests or bedheads. That it was local wood that was mostly employed to make panels can be proved by the fact that artists changed the composition of their panels according to where they were in Europe. Albrecht Durer, for example, employed poplar when he was in Italy and oak when in the Netherlands or Southern Germany. A work on poplar is therefore not likely to be English and a painting on an oak panel such as *A Protestant Allegory*, is unlikely to have been painted in Italy.

Girolamo da Treviso was an artist, a draughtsman, a woodcut designer and a military engineer. He was born *c.* 1497 in Treviso, near Venice. At around the age of 23 he is documented in Bologna and five years later was to be found in Genoa where the art historian Giorgio Vasari claims he frescoed Casa Doria, the house of an Italian *condottiero* (leader of mercenaries) and Imperial admiral to Charles V, Holy Roman Emperor. Treviso continued to Ravenna where he painted a picture in the English students' chapel in the Oratory of St Sebastiano (today only fragmentary). Henry VIII is said to have heard of his achievements and invited the artist to England. Treviso arrived in 1538 and was employed by the king as an artist and a military engineer. At the siege of Boulogne in 1544, Treviso devised a method of undermining the walls of the city and orchestrating their collapse. The city was laid low with dysentery and starvation was rife on both sides. Accounts of Treviso's death tell of him either being crushed by rubble as the walls collapsed or being hit by cannon fire. Either way, this talented polymath died in France, aged 47, in the service of Henry VIII. His picture, *A Protestant Allegory*, is one of just a few paintings that can be placed with certainty in Henry VIII's collection; it hung in the King's Privy Gallery and remains today at Hampton Court Palace.

5

THE KING'S PAINTER: HANS HOLBEIN AT HOME AND ABROAD

STRANGER, YOU WISH TO SEE PICTURES THAT PERFECTLY RESEMBLE LIFE? BEHOLD THIS WORK BY HOLBEIN'S NOBLE HAND.

NICHOLAS BOURBON

SIXTEENTH-CENTURY ENGLAND was ready for the arrival of Hans Holbein the Younger and Holbein was certainly ready for England. After a short visit in 1526, he arrived again in 1532 and by 1535 the artist from Germany had been appointed King's Painter to Henry VIII. The rapid recognition of his skills was due to the talents he had honed on the continent and, as such, his early years are key to his meteoric rise to fame in the Tudor court.

THE EARLY YEARS

Self-portrait

Hans Holbein the Younger, 1542–43, Uffizi Gallery, Florence

Holbein was born in 1497 in Augsburg, Germany. He was 12 years old in 1509 when Henry VIII was crowned king of England. Notes on his drawings indicate that he had a good level of education, could write as well as the average gentleman of his day and understand Latin.

Holbein's father, Hans Holbein the Elder, was a leading artist, and the young Holbein showed early promise. At 17, he left Augsburg for Basel, Switzerland, and there completed his earliest surviving portrait panels, the likenesses of the Burgomaster Jacob Meyer and his unhappy looking wife, Dorothea. In his tiny handwriting, Holbein has recorded on the drawing that Meyers's 'eyebrows are lighter than his hair'. The practice of writing comments on his sketches continued throughout his career and can be seen on some portraits of Henry VIII's courtiers now in the Royal Collection. For example, on the drawing of Mary, Duchess of Richmond, Holbein has inscribed the words *samet rot* (red velvet) and *schwarz felbet* (black velvet) – references made in case the sketch be worked into a portrait. Lady Mary was the daughter of Thomas Howard and thus a cousin of Anne Boleyn. She married Henry Fitzroy, the only acknowledged illegitimate son of Henry VIII.

Holbein became a citizen of Basel in 1520 and in July the same year he married Elsbeth Schmidt, a widow of a tanner with one son. Holbein continued making his living in Basel by painting altarpieces and portraits, and by creating remarkable perspectives on facades and interiors.

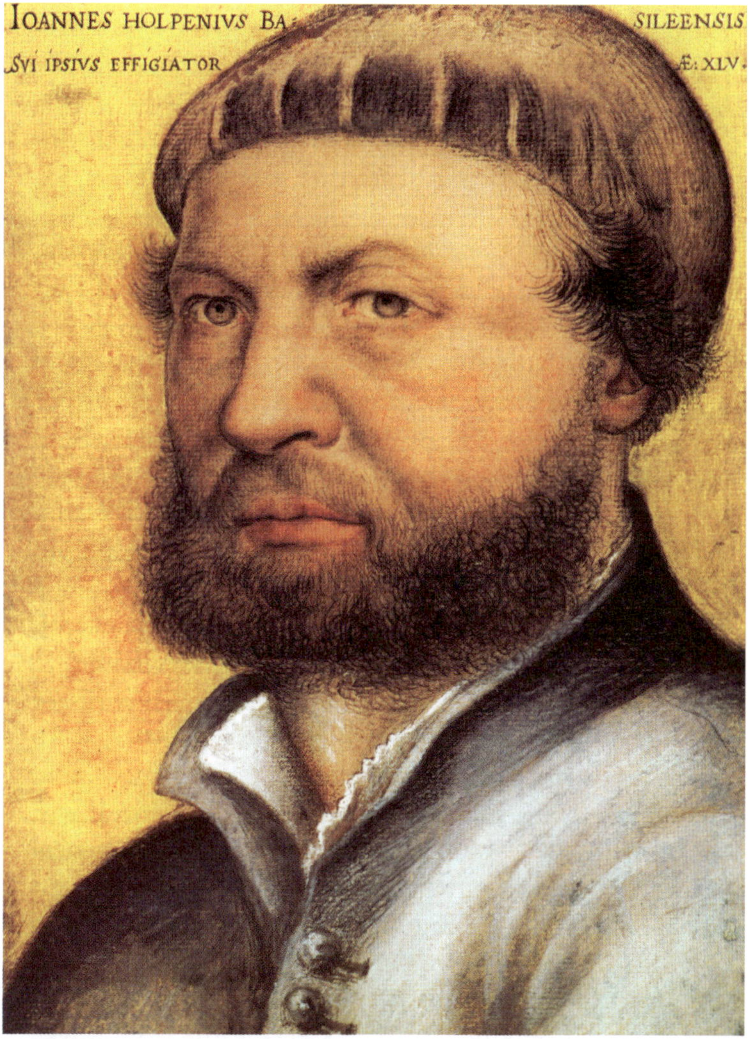

Self-portrait by Hans Holbein the Younger, aged 45. Holbein was considered the most talented portraitist of Henry's reign.

He accepted private commissions from his friend Johan Froben, the printer, and from his small portraits to his large cartoons, Holbein's skill was evident.

For the next two years, Holbein continued drawing for Froben and, occasionally, for other printers in Basel. He drew a title page for a printing of the New Testament in German, published by Adam Petri in 1523, with symbols of the Evangelists on all four corners and St Peter and St Paul on either side. Holbein contributed to a larger number of Bible editions than any other artist of the early Reformation and there has been much debate as to whether Holbein cut his own blocks for printing. He would certainly have been capable of doing so, but the Guild rules were strict, and the intrusion would not have been welcomed. The tiny 'Dance of Death' woodcuts for which Holbein is well remembered were engraved in 1523–25 by one 'Hans Lutzelburger, a form-cutter called Franck', who was one of the finest block cutters of his time.

Holbein, Johan Froben and Desiderius Erasmus of Rotterdam, the distinguished humanist scholar, were all members of the same intellectual group that admired Henry VIII for his refinement and enlightenment. It was Erasmus who wrote the letter of introduction to Thomas More that was in a few short years to bring Holbein to England.

Holbein's painting of the Council Chamber in the Rathaus (Town Hall) in Basel was interrupted due to financial and religious problems, but at the time it was considered so remarkable that he was given the nickname 'the German Apelles' after the renowned painter of ancient Greece rated 'superior' to his peers by Pliny the Elder. A façade of a house on which Holbein created a mural included the depiction of a dog that was said to be so realistic that dogs in the street would run up and bark at it, and a painted horse jumping over a balcony that shocked the passers-by below.

We know that by 1524 Holbein had painted at least three portraits of Erasmus, because in June that year Erasmus wrote to a friend in Nurnberg to say that he had sent two pictures by 'the most accomplished painter' to England and one to France. Holbein may already have been looking outside Basel for a respected patron and it is possible that one of the pictures was taken by the artist to Francis I in the hope of gaining commissions that did not materialise. The portrait of Erasmus on display today in the National Gallery in London came from Lambeth Palace and is almost certainly the one sent to William Wareham, Henry VIII's Archbishop of Canterbury.

Basel was at an important crossroads of ideas as well as trade. The Protestant Reformation here was led by Huldrych Zwingli, who had studied in Basel with Erasmus. Unfortunately for Holbein, reform was followed by the removal of religious images from churches and greatly reduced commissions for working artists. In 1526, plague infected the town, and for most of the spring and summer work was increasingly difficult to acquire.

The Painters Guild had presented the Town Council with a petition asking for work to help its members feed their families. It must have been a difficult time for Holbein; after the prestigious commissions he had been used to, he was now reduced to painting shields on an official building in the borough of Waldenburg, near Basel. It was at this time that his thoughts began to turn to the possibility of more lucrative employment elsewhere. He left Basel in 1526 to help bring the Renaissance ideas of Europe to English patrons.

FOREIGN ARTISTS

Henry's court welcomed European artists like Holbein for their superior technical skill, a trend that was passed down to the nobility and gentry. With this in mind, it is true to say that in Henry VIIIs reign, portraits of English subjects were principally 'produced through the eyes of foreigners, or through the eyes of English painters who are imitating the foreigners'. (David Piper, *The English Face*)

The most prominent artists during the Tudor period came from abroad and their large number caused complaint and resentment amongst native artists. In 1531, the scholar Sir Thomas Elyot complained that if the English wanted anything 'well paynted, kerved or embrawdred they abandon our own countraymen and resort unto straungers'. Members of the Painter-Stainers Company, founded in 1502, also habitually complained that commissions awarded to foreigners had resulted in the decay of art in England.

The Painter-Stainers Company in London was regulating seven-year apprenticeships for English painters, and so a workshop tradition may have existed in Britain, but there appear to have been few known masters to train students and no long tradition of teaching painting techniques as there was in Europe. It would take another generation before English painting was to come of age.

English nobility and gentry who travelled abroad on business would often take the opportunity of having a portrait painted in Europe and then transported home. William Paget, an advisor to Henry VIII, had his image painted by a Flemish artist, probably while he was in Brussels. Art followed trade routes and English merchants imported works of art from Europe for the home market. Only six of over thirty portraits produced in the 1540s and hanging today in the National Portrait Gallery in London, could possibly be attributed to English artists. While the reason for searching out foreign artists could be put down to fashion, it is also fair to say that the work produced by émigré artists at this time was more accomplished than that of native artists. Furthermore, after Henry VIII broke from the church of Rome, England became the preferred destination for German and Netherlandish artists of the reformed religion. And so, artists came to England from Germany, Italy and France, but principally from the Low Countries.

HOLBEIN'S FIRST VISIT TO ENGLAND

Armed with his reputation and with letters of recommendation from Erasmus, Holbein made his way to the Chelsea village home of the English lawyer and Renaissance humanist, Thomas More. Soon, Holbein had completed portraits for a range of sitters, from More himself to Bishop John Fisher, Archbishop William Wareham and Sir Henry Guildford, controller of the royal household. In addition, he painted his friend and fellow German, Nicolaus Kratzer of Munich. In his role as court astronomer to Henry VIII, Kratzer was the individual who designed the famous astronomical clock for Henry that remains installed (and keeping time) at Hampton Court Palace.

Although better known today for his portraits, Holbein also had a reputation for producing religious works, of which just one exists in the Royal Collection. Dated 1526, it has had various titles over the years and is today known as 'Noli me Tangere'. It portrays Mary Magdalene at the tomb of the risen Christ. Although united in subject matter to Holbein's eight-panelled altarpiece in Basel, the use of an oak panel suggests it was most likely painted on his arrival in England.

Holbein's employment by Sir Henry Guildford at the Greenwich Revels in 1527 is recorded in the latter's account book. Holbein was paid £4 10*s* for painting a panorama of Henry VIII's siege of Thérouanne in 1513, that was to be placed on a 'grete arche'. It was painted in a studio and brought by river to the palace by Lewis Demoron, described as a 'moulder of paper'. The picture was positioned on a gilded triumphal arch under which the king's guests passed on retiring after dinner. When entertaining French visitors, an amused Henry suggested that the party look back and observe a depiction of French defeat at English hands. Perhaps not one of his better diplomatic moments.

Following dinner, the guests attending the revels at Greenwich took their seats in the theatre for the evening's entertainment. On the ceiling was a canvas by Holbein, showing the world surrounded by the signs of the zodiac in their correct houses. Nicolaus Kratzer had acted as advisor on the characteristics of the astrological signs. It was all heavily coloured and gilded, and expense accounts detail the pigments that were used in the ceiling painting, although unfortunately the canvas is now lost, presumably discarded as unwanted scenery.

In the summer of 1528, Holbein returned to Basel to visit his family. Using some of the money that he had earned in England, he purchased a house for 300 guldens situated next door to the property owned by his friend the printer Johann Froben. Around 1531, Holbein painted a group portrait of his own family; a rather miserable looking Elsbeth along with two of their children. There is little to suggest that the marriage was a happy one, but it appears that Holbein did not shirk from his financial responsibilities. When his wife Elsbeth died around six years after Holbein, the contents of her will proved that the home was comfortable and well furnished.

The situation in Basel was still not favourable for artists. It was now a Protestant city with a hostile attitude to religious images. In a letter to Thomas More, Erasmus declared that 'the arts are freezing in this part of the world'. Instead of painting religious subjects or portraits, Holbein was forced to take design work for printers and goldsmiths, and in the early winter of 1531 he once again left in the hope of finding wealthy patrons.

HOLBEIN'S SECOND VISIT TO ENGLAND

In the three years since Holbein's last visit to England, much had changed. Sir Henry Guildford had died and so had William Wareham. Thomas More was preparing to resign his position of Lord Chancellor and Holbein's contacts and possible patrons were greatly diminished. He needed to seek commissions elsewhere, and it was to be the German population of London that first came to his aid.

Described as 'a German city and port situated in the City of London', the Steelyard comprised a body of German merchants who had formed a branch of the Hanseatic League in the English capital. London was never a Hanseatic port, but it was the largest trading post in England. In early Tudor times the Steelyard is estimated to have contributed as much as 15 per cent to the English economy by importing and exporting goods from ports of Europe. A chief export from London was English cloth and among the goods imported into London were furs, wheat, flax and – importantly for the artists of the city – wood, resin and timber.

The Steelyard headquarters was situated around where Cannon Street station is today. Its main, heavily fortified frontage was in Thames Street and it stretched along the river to Allhallows and Dowgate Street. Its charter and its accompanying privileges had been awarded by Henry III and remained unimpaired until the reign of Henry VIII's son, Edward VI, when a group of English merchants known as the Merchant Adventurers called for the liberties of the German merchants to be forfeited. Queen Elizabeth I went still further and by 1597–98 the merchants were expelled from the kingdom and their building was presented to the navy.

In the Thames Street area was an inn called – somewhat unsurprisingly – the Steelyard Tavern. For Holbein, it would have seemed a home from home. The predominant language was German, the wine was Rhenish and it was possible to eat smoked reindeer tongue and caviar. It was here that Holbein made new friends and found eager patrons in London.

THE STEELYARD PORTRAITS

The portraits Holbein painted of his Steelyard acquaintances between 1532 and 1533 rate among the most accomplished the artist produced. Seven of these portraits survive and are testament to the growing wealth of the merchant classes during the reign of Henry VIII.

George Gisze

Hans Holbein the Younger, 1532, oil on panel, Gemaldegalerie, Berlin, Germany.

Holbein's painting of the 34-year-old merchant George Gisze from Danzig is dated by the painted plaque above his head to 1532 and he is pictured sitting among the surroundings of the Steelyard. More commissions from Hanseatic merchants followed and the portrait of *Hans of Antwerp* was also completed in 1532. Like most portraits, it was painted on timber panels. Wood was inclined to warp and as the panels twisted the paint flaked off. Other panels might be damaged by flood, fire or infestation such as woodworm, and some were accidentally spoilt. Hans of Antwerp was examined in 2012 by Royal Collection Trust conservators and found to have suffered major damage within 100 years of its production. A theory is that it fell from the wall and broke into three pieces. The fragments were fixed together and the damage repainted, proving that Tudor households had the same domestic accidents as those of today.

Holbein was successfully carving a name for himself in the city when a letter arrived from the Burgomaster of Basel offering him an increased wage of 30 guldens a year to return to Basel as citizen-artist.

However, commissions in London were numerous, including *The Ambassadors*, which can be seen today in the National Gallery. *The Triumph of Riches* and *The Triumph of Poverty* were executed for the Great Hall of the now demolished Steelyard headquarters and copies can be seen in the Ashmolean Museum in Oxford. At the same time, Holbein continued to produce engravings, miniatures and designs for artefacts from jewels to cups.

One such creation was a silver standing cup for Anne Boleyn topped with her device of the falcon and a table fountain for her to present to Henry VIII at New Year 1534. It is not known if Holbein replied to the Burgomaster or not but, fully engaged with work, he stayed in London.

There were many artists who were skilled enough to decorate the royal palaces, but Holbein's talent for creating a physical presence with his work was unrivalled, and he was appointed court painter in 1535. That year, after being drawn by Holbein, the French poet Nicholas Bourbon enthused: 'Stranger, you wish to see pictures that perfectly resemble life? Behold this work by Holbein's noble hand.'

In 1536, Holbein was commissioned to paint the portrait of Henry VIII's third wife, Jane Seymour. Today, the preliminary chalk drawing is at Windsor Castle and the painting is in the Kunsthistorisches Museum in Vienna, where it has resided since 1720. It was at this time that news reached him that his old friend Erasmus had died and been buried with great honours. Within the year, Holbein was commissioned to produce one of the greatest portraits of his career; the mural of Henry VIII on the wall of the king's privy chamber in Whitehall Palace. (see chapter six). Holbein transformed the image of Henry VIII, painting him as an indubitable, self-assured leader.

On the birth of Henry's son Edward in October 1537, the king commissioned Holbein to design a cup. This was to be known as 'the Jane Seymour cup' and the preparatory drawings of it can be seen in the Bodleian Library in Oxford. An outstanding creation, this piece places Holbein amongst the most talented designers of his time. His understanding of the classical art of the goldsmith contributed to a revolution in English decorative pieces.

Jane Seymour died shortly after giving birth and Henry VIII considered marrying again. Holbein was

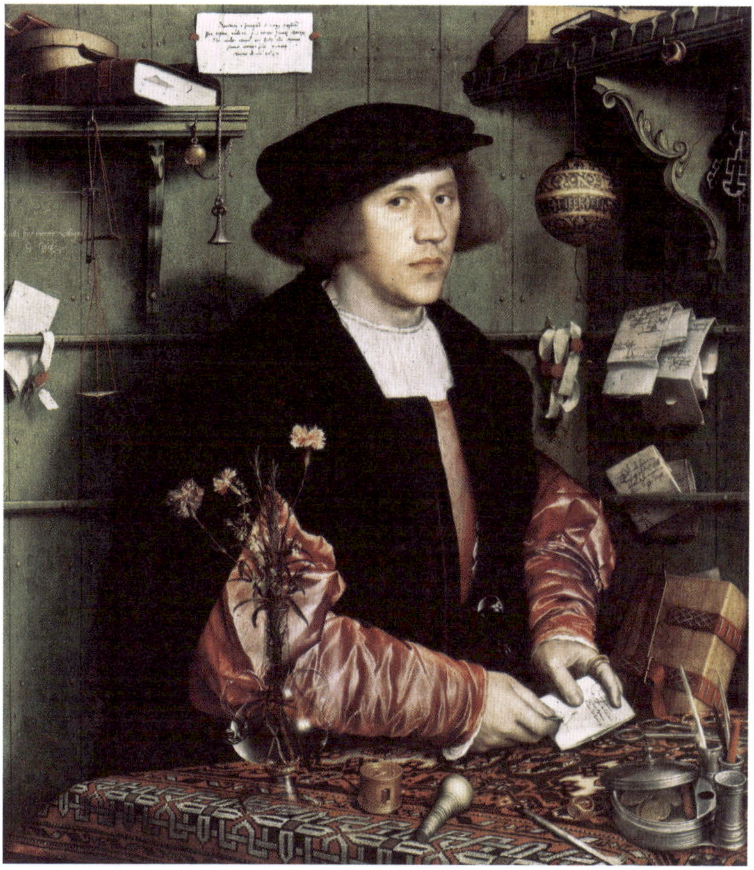

George Gisze, painted by Holbein in 1532, was a wealthy merchant and member of the Hanseatic League in London.

despatched to Brussels to produce a portrait of the daughter of Christian of Denmark: Christina, Duchess of Milan. The Duchess was the 16-year-old widow of Francis Sforza, Duke of Milan, who had died in 1535. The young girl was painted almost life size and Holbein showed her to be pretty. Whether she really gave Henry the rebuff attributed to her is unsure, but in reply to this proposal of marriage she is said to have said, 'I have but one head; had I two, one should be at your Majesty's service.'

In 1538, Holbein made a brief visit home to his family. He is likely to have taken some of the London profits with him to invest for their well-being and he may have been tempted to know more of the Burgomaster's offer to return to Basel on an increased salary. However, he was back in London before the end of the year.

On Holbein's return, documents in the National Archives reveal that the artist was awarded a licence and grant from the king to purchase 600 tons of beer. This probably indicates that the king traded with Holbein, perhaps via the influence of John Godsalve, whom the artist had known from his Steelyard days. In 1532 Holbein had drawn Godsalve in recognition of his position in the Office of the Common Meter of Precious Tissues (cloth of gold and silver). The portrait, which is still rich and vibrant in colour, remains in the Royal Collection. These are the portraits that built Holbein's reputation – and it is easy to see why. Far from being stiff portraits of medieval kings and their courtiers, Holbein has left us snapshots of real personalities, so lifelike that they almost appear to be in our presence. With fascination, we look closely into the eyes of an individual who was familiar with Henry VIII, on whose orders, many were executed.

It was customary on New Years' Day to present a gift to the king and to receive one in return. In January 1539,

Holbein offered a portrait to Henry VIII of his son Edward and, in return, the king presented him with a gilt cruse; a small two-handled pot with a cover that was made by Cornelius Hayes, one of Henry VIII's goldsmiths. The gift was worth between £3 and £5, a substantial amount to an artist earning a salary of £30 per annum. The account book of Thomas Cromwell tells us that just a few days later, on 4 January, Holbein received an additional payment of 40*s* 'by his Lord's commandement', illustrating that Holbein was still very much in demand.

Henry's marriage negotiations with the Duchess of Milan having fallen apart, Holbein was sent by the king to the Duchy of Cleves to produce a likeness of another potential bride: Anne of Cleves. The French ambassador, Charles de Marrillac wrote to Francis I to tell him that the English king had sent an excellent painter to Germany to paint the portrait of Anne. Marrillac's dispatches, although often based on gossip, are a valuable source of information about the English Court, as he worked tirelessly to keep his royal master informed.

Anne of Cleves

Hans Holbein the Younger, c. *1539, oil and tempera on parchment mounted on canvas, Louvre, Paris*

The portrait is in oil on parchment and mounted on a panel. This was unusual and suggests that Holbein painted it while in Cleves and not by later copying a sketch when back in London. Anne is wearing a headdress of cloth of gold and is facing full front with her jewelled hands clasped in front of her. Henry had already rejected one image of Anne as not revealing enough of her face, so this unobstructed pose was to give him a better idea of the lady's physical appearance.

Marrillac described Anne as 'the gentlest and kindest of Queens'. Henry's agents considered her to be 'no great beauty though not uncomely', and he was also aware that she was no linguist and was equally uneducated in music. However, Henry was enamoured by Anne's portrait and the negotiations went ahead. She arrived in England and, on New Year's Day 1540, Henry met her privately in Rochester on her journey from Dover. According to testimony from the king's companions, he was immediately disappointed with Anne, feeling that she was not as described, and he found her so unattractive that he was unable to consummate the marriage. Within a matter of months, she was living in a separate home and having to get used to the life of a single woman. The marriage was annulled, Anne was awarded a pension and addressed by the formal title of 'King's Sister'. Her life had changed enormously on the strength of one portrait by Holbein.

It was said that Henry dubbed her 'a Flanders mare', but this attribution appears to come from Bishop Gilbert Burnet in the seventeenth century. The suggestion that Holbein had flattered her in his portrait is unlikely. Without modern technology such as photography or video it is impossible to say if this portrait or any other image painted more than 500 years ago really is true to life. However, from the work of Holbein that is left to us, we know it was unusual for him to flatter his sitters and he was aware that the king required a good likeness. Henry's revulsion is most likely to have emanated from other aspects of the lady than her face.

There is no evidence that the portrait of Anne of Cleves affected Holbein's relationship with the king. Thomas Cromwell, who had arranged the marriage, was executed

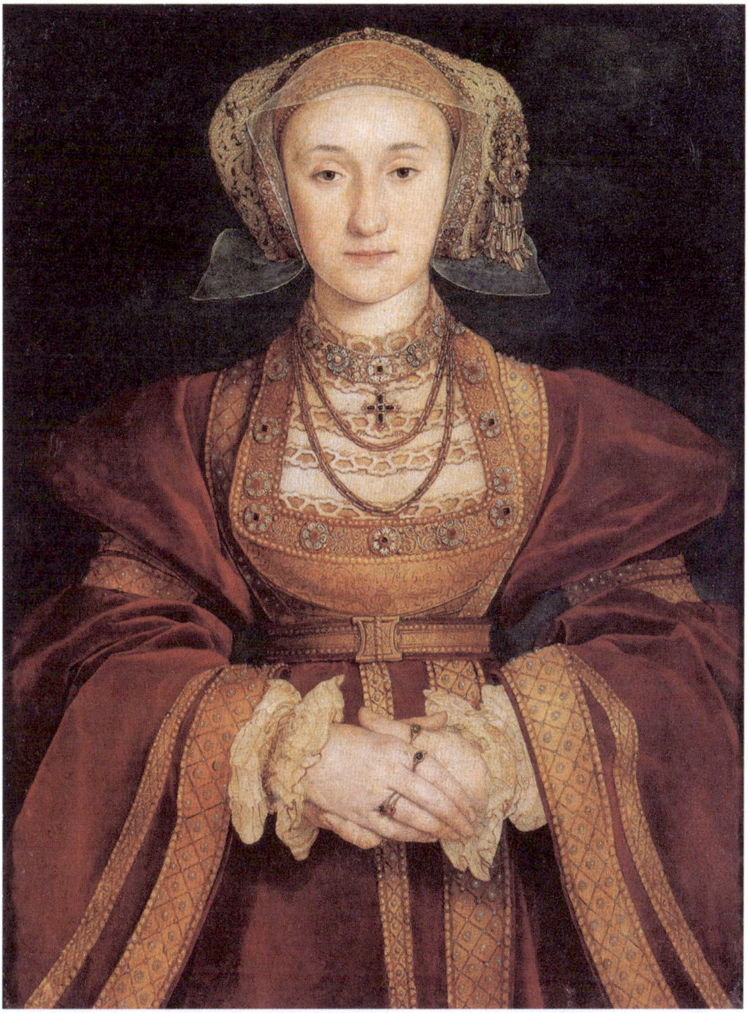

After seeing Holbein's portrait of Anne of Cleves, Henry decided to make her his fourth wife.

for treason and heresy in the summer of 1540, but Holbein survived Henry's wrath. Although there are no known commissions from the king after 1539, he continued to receive his salary until his death. The painting of Anne left the Royal Collection for that of Louis XIV of France. It was acquired by Eberhard Jabach in 1671 and is today on display in the Louvre, Paris.

Precious little solid information about Holbein remains to us, but there is mention of him in the Subsidy Roll for the City of London in 1541 that names 'Hanns Holbene' as one of the 'straungers' then residing in the Parish of Saint Andrew Undershaft.

THE DEATH OF HOLBEIN

It is recorded that Holbein died in the autumn of 1543 but we do not know the exact date or the cause. His will was found in the archives of St Paul's Cathedral in 1861 and shows that it was made on 7 October 1543. On 29 November the administration of his estate was passed to one of his executors, indicating that the artist died sometime between these two dates.

Apart from mention of a couple of debts that were to be paid by the sale of his goods, including his horse, Holbein left his worldly goods to his 'two chylder which be at nurse'. Nothing is mentioned about where the children were living, so it can only be assumed that the executor knew how to find them. The mother of the offspring in London is not named in the will, meaning that either she had already died and left the children with their nurse, or Holbein felt no responsibility for her. Another possibility is that the children were by different mothers with whom he had only ever had a passing relationship.

Plague was raging in the area where Holbein was living – so much so that the London Law Courts could not manage, and their business was transferred to St Albans. The most likely scenario is that the artist succumbed to the disease and was buried in either the Church of St Andrew Undershaft or in the nearby St Katherine Cree. However, it is unlikely the witnesses of his last will and testament would have attended his bedside amidst an outbreak of plague. Without documentation there remains the possibility that Holbein died of another quickly progressing illness. Either way, there is no grave or monument to this remarkable man who was to Henry VIII the most supremely talented artist he could ever have employed.

6

IMAGES OF HEROES: THE WHITEHALL MURAL

If it pleases you to see the illustrious images of heroes, look on these: no picture ever bore greater.

Whitehall Mural

Of Henry VIII's great houses, none was more important than Whitehall Palace, and it was here, in 1537, that Hans Holbein created his famous mural of the Tudor dynasty. Holbein's *Henry VIII* was painted directly on to the wall of the privy chamber. It was not a true fresco, which is produced on wet plaster, but a wall painting. The English climate was far too damp to support true fresco. Unfortunately, when the palace burned down in 1698 it took with it this work – the most definitive picture of an English monarch that has ever been conceived.

Henry VII, Elizabeth of York, Henry VIII and Jane Seymour

Remigius van Leemput, c. *1667, oil on canvas, Royal Collection Trust*

A preparatory drawing still exists, in the National Portrait Gallery, London, along with numerous copies by unknown artists. We are also fortunate that a small copy of the entire composition survives, painted in 1667 by Remigius van Leemput, an artist from Antwerp. This version belongs to the Royal Collection and is the only complete record of the Whitehall Mural. It was reproduced at the command of Leemput's royal master, King Charles II, from whom the artist received £150.

THE PALACE OF WHITEHALL

Whitehall was the largest palace in Europe, stretching over 23 acres from Charing Cross to Westminster Hall. Originally known as York Place, Henry VIII acquired the property after Cardinal Wolsey's fall in 1529. The name Whitehall was first recorded in 1532 and had its origins in the white stone used for the buildings. Henry spent an estimated £30,000 extending it into his main London residence, with sporting facilities, elaborate gardens, a tiltyard for jousting (now the site of Horse Guards Parade) and extensive private lodgings.

All of Henry's greater houses were built on a magnificent scale, emphasising not only the king's power but the fact that wherever he resided became the seat of government. Just like Hampton Court, Richmond and Greenwich, the new palace of Whitehall was situated on the River Thames

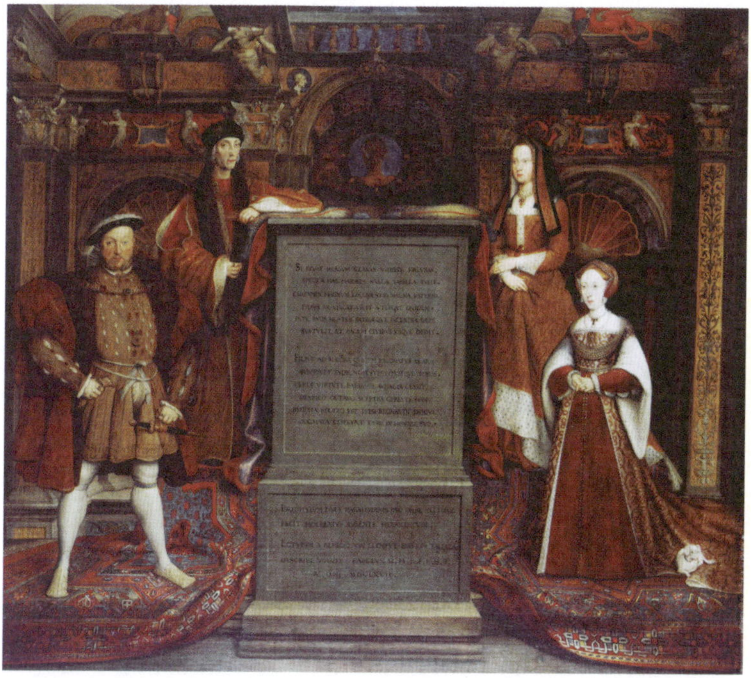

A copy of the Whitehall Mural made during the reign of Charles II. The original was painted by Holbein in 1537 and destroyed by a fire in 1698.

which provided easy transportation by barge. Many of these palaces were drawn by the Flemish artist Anthony van Wyngaerde in the middle of the sixteenth century, and this has left us a unique visual record. We can see the common features of Tudor architecture: tall gatehouses and crenelated turrets, stone mullions, bay windows and elaborately carved chimney pots.

All the palaces had brightly painted exteriors, perhaps garish to modern eyes, which would have made them look to us like Disneyland castles. The interiors were also richly decorated, with furnishings becoming even more splendid as one entered the king's apartments. The presence chamber contained a throne and canopy of estate, and here the king would receive formal delegations from those entitled to come into his presence. Henry's inner sanctum was the privy chamber, a private room beyond, to which access was strictly controlled. Few had right of entry to this magnificent room and its connected lodgings, where the king conducted his private life. It was staffed by senior courtiers, who attended to Henry's personal needs: washing and dressing him, and serving his meals. The 'privy chamber' was thus also a term for this body of privileged staff, who included gentleman, ushers, grooms and pages. It is certain that the privy chamber at Whitehall would have been lavishly furnished with tapestries, floor carpets and a chair of estate, and it was here – at the heart of his power base – that Henry planned a painting that would dominate the room.

No contract survives for the Whitehall Mural, but it was commissioned in the short period between Henry's marriage to Jane Seymour in May 1536 and her death in October 1537. Hans Holbein had painted the king before: a small picture on panel that is today in the collection of the Thyssen-Bornemisza museum in Madrid and is the only portrait of Henry VIII bearing the artist's signature. But the Whitehall painting was on an entirely different scale and would become the standard likeness of Henry VIII. The commission was probably requested when Queen Jane became pregnant. It measured 3m x 4m, and portrayed Henry with Jane and his parents, Henry VII and Elizabeth of York, grouped around a marble plinth. By painting the figures on to the wall, Holbein added them to the fabric of the building, as a splendid backdrop to the king's physical presence in the chamber. It is likely that Henry's intention was to leave a lasting statement, devised in the year that his expected son would be born, and painted after the most difficult year of his reign.

THE YEAR 1536

Early in 1536, the king had a bad jousting accident that may have caused him to reflect on his own mortality. Anne Boleyn miscarried and, after twenty-seven years on the throne, he still had no male heir. He had cut England off from Catholic Christendom and begun to close down the monasteries, but political disaster had struck with the rebellion known as 'The Pilgrimage of Grace'. Henry was no longer the athletic youth of the past; his diseased legs were causing him increasing pain and would soon turn him into a semi-invalid. It is possible the fall aggravated the leg ulcers and varicose veins that he had suffered since the 1520s. It may also have deepened Henry's concerns about his lack of a male heir. Added to this, in July 1536, his acknowledged illegitimate son, Henry Fitzroy, died of tuberculosis, aged 17.

The loss of Anne's child had ensured her downfall and Jane Seymour's rise. From 1536 Henry courted Jane openly, promoting her brothers at court and sending her expensive gifts. Anne was arrested for high treason in May and sent to the Tower of London, where she was put on trial. It is likely that her fall was engineered by Thomas Cromwell, acting in accordance with Henry's wish to free himself. On the morning of Friday, 19 May, Anne was executed within the Tower precincts, although historians have long viewed the charges against her – adultery, incest and plotting to kill the king – to be unconvincing. This destruction of Henry's second queen, combined with his mistreatment of the first, began to cement the king's reputation in Europe as a ruthless and undesirable husband, as witnessed by the later comments of Christina, Duchess of Milan, that she would marry the King of England if she had an extra head.

Henry and Jane were betrothed on 20 May, the day after Anne's execution, and they married at the Palace of Whitehall on 30 May. Jane was around 28 – only six or seven years younger than Anne – and the Imperial ambassador, Chapuys described her as 'of middle stature and no great beauty, so fair that one would call her rather pale than otherwise'. But Jane was, by all appearances, gentle and compassionate, in contrast to her ambitious predecessor. Henry would in years to come remember her as 'the fairest, the most discreet, and the most meritorious of all his wives.' It is possible that she reminded him of his mother, Elizabeth of York and that, like Elizabeth, she would be virtuous, pious, gentle and, above all, fruitful. Jane's family were known for their fertility and her motto as queen was 'Bound to obey and serve'. Henry's expectations – set out so clearly in the mural – were finally fulfilled on 12 October 1537. Throughout the realm, people greeted the birth of a male heir with joy and relief; 'Te Deums' were sung in churches and bonfires lit. Queen Jane, appearing to recover quickly from the birth, sent out personally signed letters announcing the birth of 'a Prince, conceived in most lawful matrimony between my Lord the King's Majesty and us'. The queen, however, fell ill on 23 October from presumed postnatal complications, and died the following night. Henry VIII wrote to Francis I of France that 'Divine Providence ... hath mingled my joy with bitterness of the death of her who brought me this happiness'. Certainly, Jane Seymour had occupied a very particular place in the heart of Henry VIII and he was genuinely grief-stricken. Not only had she died after giving birth to his longed-for son but her death may have revived painful recollections of his mother, who also died as the result of childbirth.

If Jane Seymour was pregnant when Holbein started the commission for the Whitehall Mural, she was certainly dead by the time of its completion. Henry VII, Elizabeth of York and Jane Seymour – who were all deceased – are depicted looking into the composition, and away from the viewer, while Henry VIII holds our gaze, as the only living figure represented. Holbein may have experimented with different angles and the change may also have come about after the king quashed the Pilgrimage of Grace, emphasising his triumph. Henry is depicted standing fast against all adversaries, whether it be the Pope, his own subjects or other European powers. He stands like a man in armour, ready to fight – for England now stands outside Catholic Europe, with its own church and new forms of worship. To justify and maintain his position Henry will increase the size and fighting capacity of his navy, improve his army, and build fortifications for defence. Whatever the reason for the change to full face, it is a clever device to grab the viewer's attention.

Cartoon for the Whitehall Mural

Hans Holbein the Younger, c. *1536–37, ink and watercolour, National Portrait Gallery, London*

THE CARTOON

One of Holbein's original preparatory drawings, known as a cartoon (or pattern), has survived; showing us the left-hand side of the mural and – importantly – Henry VIII. The cartoon is made from several sheets of paper pieced together. Following the outline of the drawing, small holes were made through the paper. This was known as 'pricking'. The paper pattern was then held to the wall and 'pounced', a method by which chalk or charcoal dust was brushed or blown through the holes in the paper and onto the wall. The cartoon was then removed, the charcoal dots on the wall were joined up and the preliminary sketch was filled out and finished. Painting could then begin.

Henry's head is on a separate sheet of paper, attached to the larger drawing at the neck, and he appears three-quarter face. However, in the copy by Remigius van Leemput the king is turned from a three-quarter angle to a more arresting stance, with Henry confronting the viewer face on. This was an unusual pose for any royal portrait, and if the Leemput version is taken as a faithful copy, Holbein's mural was innovative.

IMAGE OF POWER

Holbein's image was also the first life-size, full-length portrait of a monarch to be produced in England, and

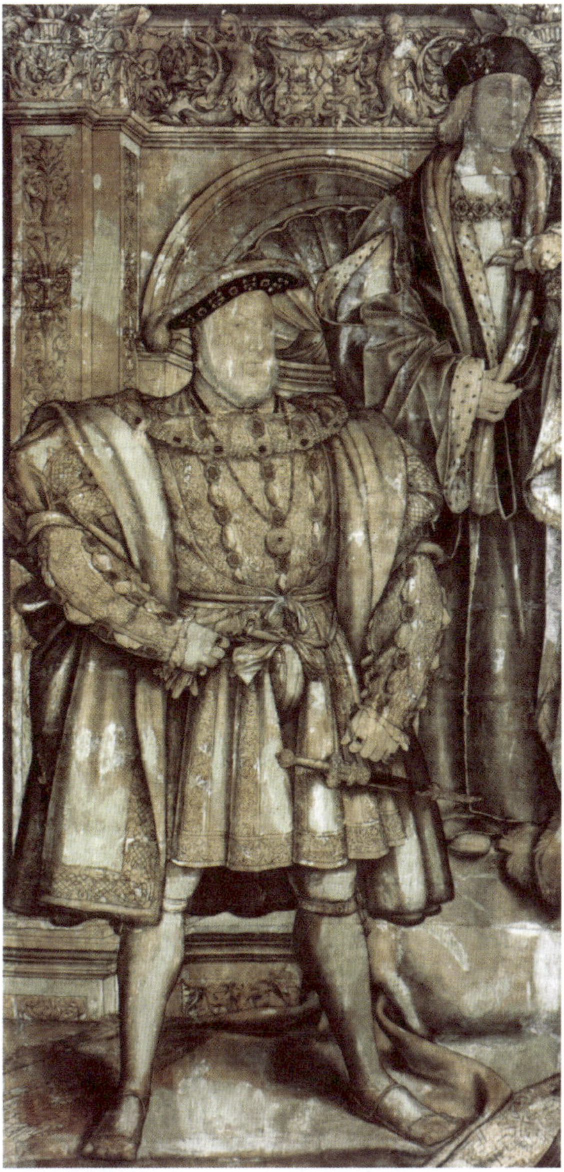

An original preparatory drawing for the Whitehall Mural, known as a cartoon, has survived.

among the first to be painted in Europe. With feet planted firmly apart, he glares down at us with total authority. Henry was 46 at the time, which was old by Tudor standards, and his legs were troubling him. Yet in the picture he appears strong and healthy. The codpiece, at the very centre of the composition, proclaims the king's virility and hints at the continuation of the dynasty. His imposing stance suggests that he is at the peak of his powers, one hand clutching his dagger, giving the impression of being ready for action at a moment's notice. We know that Holbein deliberately distorted Henry's physique and his legs have been elongated to make him look slimmer. A surviving piece of armour made for the king in 1540 proves that his legs were noticeably shorter in reality. Padded shoulders add to Henry's bulk and may also explain why Holbein chose to lengthen the royal legs, to preserve balance in the composition. His clothing is sumptuous and costly, with every jewel demonstrating wealth and magnificence. For Henry, clothes sent an important message, and he was the first monarch to use his wardrobe for spectacular political effect.

In 1519, the Venetian ambassador, Sebastian Guistinian, had described him as 'the best dressed sovereign in the world'. The king's dress represented the affluence of the country and any monarch who underspent would be considered lacking. An inventory of Henry's wardrobe in 1521 estimates its value at £10,380, which equates to almost £4 million today. The right clothing and jewels could supply an instantly recognisable regal image, without the need for a crown, and Henry was known to flaunt his jewellery. It is likely that the jewels that Holbein so carefully reproduced were entrusted to the artist on separate occasions, rather than taking up any of the king's time. Fine details on the clothing could likewise be copied from the garments themselves, and they would be supplied by Henry's gentlemen of the Great Wardrobe. The same department would have provided the intricate Turkish carpet, which is draped over the stone plinth and trails down the steps to where the king stands. It adds much to the rich decoration of the setting and proclaims his status. Carpets were a luxury only the richest people could afford and they were generally much too expensive to put on the floor.

PROPAGANDA

The mural has often been described as propaganda for the Tudor dynasty, created to extol the virtues of two great kings and the coalition of the Plantagenet royal houses. Here was a family who would ensure domestic peace between the warring claims of the red rose of Lancaster and the white rose of York. Henry VIII was the physical embodiment of that union and his duty was to continue his line.

It was also an opportunity for Henry to outshine his father, and he clearly ranked his historical role as higher than that of Henry VII. The long Latin inscription, at the centre of the picture, emphasises Henry VIII's defeat of his rebellious subjects and his supremacy over the Roman Catholic Church. His motivation was to prove more successful than his father, although the historical facts suggest otherwise.

The first Tudor king had won the crown by risking his life on the battlefield at Bosworth (though, interestingly, he never felt the need to commission a painting of the victory). His son craved glory in battle and the crown of France, but his military campaigns had all proved costly and of indifferent success. Henry VII had established a secure dynasty, while his son's life had become dominated by the need for a male heir. Henry VII had left a full treasury, which would soon be depleted by a son who spent extravagantly to impress and compete with far more powerful European monarchs. But the inscription tells us Henry VIII was greater:

> If it pleases you to see the illustrious images of heroes, look on these: no picture ever bore greater. The great debate, competition and great question is whether father or son is the victor. For both, indeed, were supreme. The father triumphed over his foes and brought his people lasting peace. The son was born to a greater destiny ... presumptuous popes were forced to yield before him ... and true religion was established.

The use of the past tense is revealing: Henry expects the painting to live on, long after his death. The dynasty was now assured and he was presenting himself and his father as powerful examples for his son to follow. It is also clear that Henry wishes to be remembered by posterity as a great religious reformer. Leading his people to the 'true religion' was even more important than military triumph.

Henry's confrontational pose makes him seem more forceful than his father, even though the figure of Henry VII is elevated. Some who saw it at Whitehall Palace found the image rather terrifying. The artist and art historian Karl van Mander wrote that it 'was so lifelike that the spectator felt abashed, annihilated in its presence'. He also mentions in his *Lives of the Artists* of 1604 that: 'The King's affection for Holbein increased, and he favoured him more and more, as the artist served him so well according to his wishes.'

COPIES

Holbein's design managed to capture both a recognisable likeness of Henry and at the same time present him as a supreme leader, cleverly turning obesity and bulk into something powerful and menacing. The likeness was endlessly copied and became the most popular and enduring portrait of the king. A portrait of Edward VI in the National Portrait Gallery, believed to have been painted following his accession, mimics the strong pose of his father in the Whitehall Mural. Copies which survive today are known as 'after Holbein' – in other words, by a follower of Hans Holbein. It is these copies, rather than the original (which few would see), which have made Henry VIII our most recognisable English king. The success of Holbein's portrait as a tool for propaganda, whether employed consciously or not, is clear when you compare it with earlier portraits of the king.

During his reign Henry used his portraits to further his diplomatic ends by sending them as political gifts and to cement relations and alliances. They were also used by nobility and courtiers to flatter and affirm their loyalty to the king. Full-length copies were soon produced and Holbein's likeness of the king circulated between artists' workshops both before and after his death, as a pattern for smaller paintings such as those commissioned as part of sets for display in long galleries. These later images were painted in large numbers to celebrate the reign of Henry VIII. Many still exist, derived from the original, but they were not the work of Hans Holbein.

(A large number of Holbein's portrait drawings were assembled after his death into the 'Great Boke'. These may be the drawings mentioned in the 1547 inventory of Edward VI and referred to as 'a booke of paternes for phiosioneamyes'.)

Two of the most refined full-length copies date from the 1540s: the paintings at Petworth House, West Sussex, and in the Walker Art Gallery, Liverpool. These are the only reproductions which contain elements of the background architecture shown in the mural copy by Leemput. The Walker version was probably commissioned by a senior courtier declaring his allegiance to Henry and may have been painted by an artist who had access to the cartoon for the mural scheme. As described earlier, Holbein was able to transfer portrait drawings using the pouncing method, a technique that meant he could make labour-saving copies of drawings. It is possible that he entrusted other artists to complete painted portraits, although there is no evidence to suggest that Holbein employed assistants in London. He was an alien in the city until 1541 and as such it was illegal for him to employ others, although his relationship with the king may have led to this being overlooked. The Petworth copy has a scallop-shell niche behind Henry's head and the folded carpet that can be seen in the original. However, differences in the depiction of Henry's clothes and the furnishings suggest that in both versions the artists were not reliant on either the cartoon or the mural.

The Flemish artist William Scrots copied Henry's assertive stance several times for portraits of his son and successor, Edward VI. An accomplished version of Scrots's work was purchased by Queen Victoria in 1882, for the Royal Collection. Painted full-length, like his father, Edward stands within a marble interior, wearing a costly black doublet, heavily padded to enhance his shoulders; his right hand holds gloves, his left holds the end of his belt at his waist. The original, from which this derives, is thought to have been commissioned in 1550 during the marriage negotiations between Edward VI and the eldest daughter of Henri II of France.

The identities of most artists who copied Holbein's Henry are unknown. However, there are two portraits that we know of by Hans Eworth, one of Holbein's most gifted successors. A copy hangs at Trinity College, Cambridge, with the inscription 'HE' in the lower left corner, and there is also a version at Chatsworth House. Interestingly, the Cavendish family of Chatsworth also once owned the Whitehall Mural cartoon. Full-length portraits of Henry were produced into the early seventeenth century, such as those at Belvoir, Parham, St Bartholomew's Hospital and in the Royal Collection. In 1737 George Vertue produced a watercolour of van Leemput's painting, 200 years after Holbein had created the original painting. Vertue's copy is not entirely faithful to van Leemput's painting; he did not include the codpiece worn by Henry VIII in van Leemput's copy and in the original mural.

In 1776 Sir Joshua Reynolds created a humorous portrait entitled *Master Crewe as Henry VIII* in which a 3-year-old boy is shown in a parody of Henry's outfit and stance. Reynolds copied the sixteenth-century clothing as 'fancy dress' and omitted the codpiece. According to the antiquarian Horace Walpole, Reynolds had reduced the 'swaggering and colossal haughtiness' of the original image to the 'boyish jollity of Master Crewe'.

In 1933, Holbein's likeness stepped out of the painting and onto celluloid when Charles Laughton starred in *The Private Life of Henry VIII*. The production was an international success and won Laughton an Academy Award for Best Actor. He successfully brought the famous visual image of Henry to life – although his portrayal of a lecherous glutton, tossing chicken bones over his shoulder, was far from accurate.

Few monarchs have matched Henry VIII's ability to impose his image on posterity, from wall painting to cinema screen. He is the only English king whom the vast majority of people, from all over the world, would recognise at first sight. Our modern view of him does not derive from any paintings executed before 1537 but from the compelling image that Holbein created at Whitehall Palace. It was precisely what was required by Henry to portray him as God's deputy on earth – an enduring image of brutal, autocratic power.

7

MAGNIFICENCE AND PROPAGANDA: THE ABRAHAM TAPESTRIES

And God said unto Abraham, Thou shalt keep my covenant

Genesis 12:24

The first Tudor king, Henry VII, was eager to assert his royal authority and spent great sums on the royal palaces at Richmond and Greenwich. He was also fully aware of the importance of tapestries, but his son Henry VIII surpassed him in both, having more than fifty great houses and an unrivalled collection of weavings by the end of his reign.

THE ABRAHAM TAPESTRIES

The Sacrifice of Isaac

Pieter Coecke van Aelst, 1540–43, wool and silk, Royal Collection Trust

Abraham, whose story is taken from Genesis 12:24, was the founder of the Hebrew nation, with God's covenant continuing through his son, Isaac. In the panel *The Sacrifice of Isaac* we see God testing Abraham's faith by commanding him to take Isaac into the land of Moriah and sacrifice him. Isaac carries wood for the ceremony and his father bears hot coals. Isaac turns to his father and asks him, 'where is the lamb for the burnt offering?' To which his father replies, 'God will provide a lamb'. The sacrifice is about to take place, with Abraham holding the knife at his son's throat, when an angel swoops down and grasps Abraham's hair to prevent him from taking any further action. In the top left of the tapestry a lamb comes out of the forest and Abraham offers it as a sacrifice in place of Isaac. One of the servants beside the mule looks up in amazement and points to the angel.

In the top centre is a stretched animal skin and a cartouche that reads in Latin, 'Abraham at God's command sacrifices his only begotten son, Isaac'. Interestingly, four letters at the bottom left of the inscription in the cartouche are not woven into the fabric but painted on, most likely to cover a mistake by the weavers. Considering that these were probably among the most valuable and costly set of tapestries ever undertaken in the Kempeneer workshop, one can only guess at the fate of the weaver!

During the reign of Henry VIII, tapestry design changed from the static, flat and decorative medieval style to a

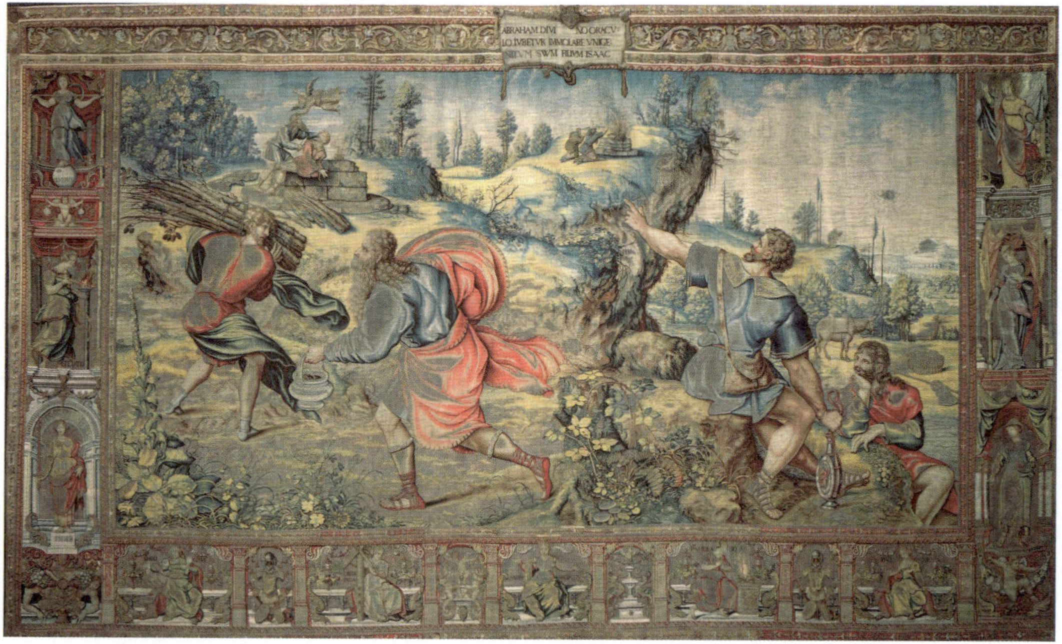

The Sacrifice of Isaac, one of ten tapestry panels from the life of the prophet Abraham.

more Renaissance-inspired composition in which movement and storytelling are depicted. In medieval tapestries, characters often had their names woven into the design and the story told in a text above or below the main panel. The arrival of the Renaissance brought a lively narrative and movement that made explanation unnecessary. The designer of this tapestry, Bernaert van Orly, has taken the decorative details of Netherlandish design and introduced into it a narrative including muscular Italianate figures in the style of Michelangelo.

Details such as the hair and beard of Abraham, the veins in the arm of the man in blue or even Abraham's toes, reveal the immense skill of the weaver. The nap on the fur bag held by the man in blue has the appearance of being worn with constant use. It is worth noting again that these remarkable images are not painted, nor embroidered, but woven on a loom. The skill is evident in the details of this composition and – half a millennia after their production – these tapestries are still hanging in the royal palace for which they were commissioned.

Around the borders of the tapestries can be seen the figures of vices and virtues. The faithful servant or the dutiful wife can contemplate the qualities displayed – *Constantia* (steadfastness), *Fides* (Faith), *Obedientia* (obedience) or *Immolatio* (sacrifice) – and the relevance of the figures to their own lives. One hundred and ten personifications are featured in the ten panels of the Abraham tapestries, and they are the first known set in which the borders are not solely for decoration but were designed to be an integral part of the tapestry.

This set is the first weaving of these designs but not the only ones. During the 1540s, Willem de Kempeneer owned the cartoons and made further copies from them. Two other weavings survive: in the Spanish royal collection in

Madrid and in the former Hapsburg collection in Vienna. Although both are high-quality weavings, neither contain the silver and gilt metal of Henry VIII's version.

At the Tudor court, the medium of tapestry far outshone that of painting or fresco. Henry VIII's palaces were decorated throughout with tapestries and he owned more than 300 sets of wall hangings made up of three or more panels. Twenty gold woven sets were acquired by Henry himself and he inherited a further 500 from Cardinal Wolsey. Less than twenty of Cardinal Wolsey's collection of over 600 tapestries can today be identified, along with a handful of armorials that are in contemporary collections. Wolsey owned a greater number of moderate-quality hangings than high-quality Brussels weavings, and tapestries from both Henry's and Wolsey's collection disappeared from the Royal Collection in the seventeenth century.

At a time when the richer nobility in England might own fifty tapestries, and the richest 100, Wolsey's large collection, principally of religious subjects, is testament to his great wealth. The appropriations Henry made during the dissolution of the monasteries extended his collection still further, and at his death, the king owned 2,450 weavings. If laid end to end, his tapestry collection would have unfolded to more than 4 miles of high-quality coloured images.

Henry VIII spent lavishly on these costly textiles, which would remain the pre-eminent art form in England throughout the sixteenth century. Although no documentation has so far come to light, *The Story of Abraham* tapestries were almost certainly commissioned by Henry VIII. They are so rich and expensive that it is highly unlikely that a workshop would have woven them on the chance of finding a buyer. Furthermore, we have some evidence from Henry's Great Wardrobe, which was responsible for the care of all textiles, including tapestries.

An account book belonging to the Wardrobe Keeper shows a payment in 1544 to the royal tailors for lining two sets of tapestries, one of them being *The Story of Abraham.* This identification is certain because there was only one Abraham set.

To be a magnificent prince entailed owning a sumptuous tapestry collection, and for Henry VIII, tapestries were principally employed as a tool for ostentation. Easily rolled up for transportation, they provided almost immediate comfort and splendour on reaching their destination, where they were hung for celebrations and for official business. A month before Henry departed for the Field of the Cloth of Gold in 1520, his Lord Chamberlain was already engaged in transporting the richest tapestries to France. Fifty-two loads were taken to Calais to embellish the temporary palace constructed at the English camp at Guines. Henry was aware that Francis I had an equally extravagant tapestry collection and competition between the two kings was always fierce. The lack of any records concerning the collection of Francis means a comparison is hard to make, but he was known to have spent large sums on tapestries designed by the Italian artists Raphael and Giulio Romano – and King Henry VIII did not like to be outshone.

PROPAGANDA

Both Henry VIII and his father used luxurious tapestries to promote their religious and political agendas. Tapestries were useful in this respect: they could tell stories and disperse moral guidance, allowing the owner to identify himself with great historic, religious and mythological figures. In the context of the English court, tapestries played a greater part in promoting the Reformation than paintings or engravings. Produced in the 1520s, *The Triumphs of Petrarch* series from Cardinal Wolsey's collection was inspired by Petrarch's poem *I Trionfi* and reflects a taste for humanist themes. In 1542, Henry acquired a seven-piece set depicting *The Triumphs of the Gods* of which two pieces survive today at Hampton Court Palace: *The Triumphs of Bacchus* and *The Triumphs of Hercules*. As a Roman god interpreted during the Renaissance as the embodiment of Christian fortitude, Hercules fitted well into Henry's agenda of self-identification.

It is notable that Henry's tapestry collection depicts classical subjects, rather than the religious schism on display in paintings such as *A Protestant Allegory*. This is partly because Henry was restricted from commissioning hangings with an anti-Catholic message as the leading tapestry workshops were in the domain of Charles V, Holy Roman Emperor, who was a staunch Catholic. Charles was also Katherine of Aragon's nephew and he supported his aunt against Henry in the sensitive matter of their divorce.

PRODUCING A TAPESTRY

The process of acquiring a set of tapestries called for patience. In the period between ordering *The Story of Abraham* tapestries *c*. 1540 and taking delivery of them a few years later, Henry VIII's circumstances had changed dramatically. He had married Anne of Cleves at the beginning of 1540 and obtained an annulment within six months. A month later, he wed the teenaged Katherine Howard. After eighteen months of marriage Henry signed the order for his young wife's execution following charges of adultery. In July 1543, Henry was joined in marriage, at Hampton Court Palace, with his sixth and last wife, Katherine Parr. So, when the tapestries finally arrived *c*. 1543/44 Henry had experienced three more marriages and was in declining health. He was only able to enjoy his magnificent acquisition for a short time before his death in 1547.

On electing to invest in a set of tapestries, the first decision for the patron was to determine how many tapestries were required – a set being usually between two and ten. He must then choose the subject matter and find his artist. At this stage, the artist would usually paint a series of small pictures or sketches of each tapestry for the patron's approval. Any changes in subject or content would be made at this stage.

Once the composition had been approved by the patron, the artist's paintings were transferred onto *cartone*, thick paper of the same dimensions as the intended tapestry, in this case 488cm x 792cm (16ft x 26ft). The spectacular cartoons by Raphael entitled *The Acts of the Apostles* are rare surviving examples of this ephemeral artform. They used to hang at Hampton Court Palace but today they can be seen at the Victoria and Albert Museum in London.

The Abraham tapestries were most likely conceived by Bernaert van Orly, the first Northern European tapestry designer to incorporate Renaissance elements into his work. Van Orly died a year into the project and so the cartoons were executed by Pieter Coecke van Aelst, an independent tapestry designer who had been part of van Orley's circle. According to Karel van Mander, van Aelst had been apprenticed to van Orley and had spent time in Italy where he had studied art and sculpture.

With the cartoon finished, the final step in creating a cycle of tapestries was to choose a workshop to weave them. During the reign of Henry VIII there was not a huge choice of specialist weavers capable of creating tapestries of the extremely high standard or size of the Abrahams.

Most of the workshops were situated in Brussels, where a large part of the city was involved in tapestry creation. In the case of this set, they were woven in the workshop of Willem de Kempeneer, who was among the most pre-eminent of weavers in the city.

A tapestry is woven by hand on a loom where the warps (strings) are stretched either vertically (high warp) or horizontally (low warp). A low warp loom was the most popular in the early sixteenth century: it was quicker to weave, the pattern was more closely observed and more intricate designs could be produced. Workshop masters needed to be entrepreneurial; they provided space to accommodate a loom for each panel of tapestry and to pay the wages for the working weavers over the period of two years or more that it took to complete and deliver a tapestry set. It is assumed that all the craftsman involved in producing tapestries were men because only male names are recorded. Although, of course, many weavers remain anonymous, it appears there were few, if any, female weavers.

With the looms set up and the weavers employed, the process could begin. The cartoon was cut into strips, probably by the weavers, and placed behind the strings of the low-warp loom. The weaver then had a close view and could clearly copy the pattern in front of him. (The cartoon was not necessarily cut into regular sizes because cutting through a face or body would be avoided.) The weaver worked from the back of the tapestry, so the design he copied would be reversed. The cartoon makers had to anticipate this in their compositions by reversing the scene for it to appear correctly when woven. Looking at cartoons for religious tapestries, for example, the Raphael cartoons, it can look odd that Christ is blessing with the left hand, instead of the right – but in the finished product it is corrected.

Each weaver was paid according to his skill. The weaver of the sky was not paid as highly as the weaver of faces or bodies, so if a weaver's strip of *cartone* included a face and his qualifications only permitted him to weave the sky then another more skilled colleague would replace him for that part of the design. The incredible talent of all the craftsmen is evidenced by the fact that we do not see the effect of all these different hands at work – we look at one, beautifully uniform, piece of tapestry.

Producing a tapestry was extremely labour intensive. An experienced weaver could produce one square metre of coarse wool tapestry or half a metre of fine tapestry a month. *The Story of Abraham* set would take thirty weavers around eighteen months to finish. This does not include the time taken to set up the loom, design the cartoons or prepare the tapestry for travelling.

The quality of a tapestry relied on a number of things: the standard of the cartoon from which it derived, the skill of the weavers to follow the design and the fineness of the weave. *The Story of Abraham* tapestries were woven at a fine eight warps to the centimetre, meaning the weaver had to pass through eight 'strings' to produce one centimetre of tapestry. The grade of the material from which the tapestry was made also had an enormous effect on the price. A silk tapestry cost around four times the price of one woven in coarse wool and the addition of gilt or silver thread further raised the price at least twenty times.

The best wool came from England or Spain, the highest-grade silk was purchased from Italy or Spain and the silver or gilt thread came from Venice or Cyprus. Costing at least £1,500, a set of tapestries of the exceptional quality of *The Story of Abraham* was more costly than the building and fitting of a battleship like the *Mary Rose*.

Though high-grade tapestry production during the reign of Henry VIII centred on Brussels, the sales and funding of tapestry most often took place in Antwerp. From the 1530s the names of various Antwerp merchants appear regularly in the accounts of the English court. Peter van Walle was granted a licence to export luxury goods, including tapestries, into England on condition that Henry VIII had first choice of his wares. Henry chose a rich tapestry bed from van der Walle for the young Prince Edward, but no further details concerning the bed are available to us.

As Brussels tapestries became more and more popular, so the quality was open to compromise and shortcuts were taken to speed production. Areas not woven as part of the design were fraudulently coloured with paint or crayon, and tapestries that had been woven in other areas of production were promoted as woven in Brussels. In 1528, the Brussels guild introduced a regulation to prevent these illegal practices. It stated that any tapestry over 6 Ells (2.81m) should have two marks woven into the selvage (the edge or border) to indicate that it had passed an inspection by the guild officers.

Before the sixteenth century, tapestries from Brussels had been marked with a lead or a wax seal but these had proved too easy to dishonestly remove. The stricter regulations called for two 'B's (for the province of Brabant and, within it, the city of Brussels) separated by a red shield to be woven on one lower edge of the tapestry with the weaver's mark on the opposite edge. These marks can be clearly seen on the selvages of the Abraham tapestries. Once inspected by guild officers their details were entered in a register, although even with these strict regulations, the retouching of tapestries still seems to have taken place. Guild regulations stipulated fines and penalties for master weavers who left Brussels to take their learned skills elsewhere. Unfortunately, the Brussels tapestry guild records, which could have answered so many burning questions concerning these artefacts, were lost in 1695.

STORY AND MEANING

In *The Story of Abraham* tapestries, Henry was presenting himself to his subjects as a prophet and he saw the story of Abraham and Isaac as a parallel for himself and his young son, Edward. Prince Edward was born in 1537, and in an era of high child mortality it would have been logical for Henry to wait for a certain time to ensure that his son would survive babyhood before commissioning these tapestries *c.* 1540. They were received and lined by the Great Wardrobe when the young prince was 7 years old. Through the design of these tapestries, Henry was referring to the Tudor sacral line that linked him directly to God.

When new, the tapestry would have gleamed in the candlelight. The colours were vibrant and bright – possibly too garish for modern tastes – but over the years the silver and gold thread has oxidised and is today seen as large areas of grey.

If the front of the tapestry appears faded, it can be a surprise to see the reverse of the weaving which gives an idea of the brightness of the original colours. An experiment some years ago aimed to give the modern viewer the experience of seeing the tapestries as Henry VIII would have seen them. By taking light readings from the front of the tapestry and repeating the process on the colours underneath the selvages, it became possible to ascertain exactly how much colour had been lost. The difference in depth between the two readings was then created in the form of a 35mm slide that could be projected onto the tapestry, creating a level of colour that members of the Tudor court would have taken for granted.

CONSERVATION

In the sixteenth century these tapestries would have been cleaned by rubbing them with bread, which proved to be an effective method of removing dust and dirt. It would be an eco-friendly way of doing so today but for the problem of attracting mice! If an infestation of insects is suspected, the tapestries are rolled up, sealed in plastic containers and frozen. After time in extremely low temperatures, the tapestries can be unrolled and rehung, leaving the bodies of the invading insects inside the container and the tapestries free from harmful chemicals.

They are thoroughly dusted yearly and frequently monitored for light damage, humidity and anything that might cause damage. Considering the design was produced using vegetable dyes, it is remarkable that an image is still visible. All cleaning procedures on these 500-year-old weavings will leave their mark and so wet cleaning of a tapestry will take place only in cases of absolute necessity. It will be laid flat over a vacuum board and sprayed with water containing just a trace of detergent. After rinsing, it will be left until it is completely dry before being moved and rehung with the aid of a modern-day invention: the hook-and-loop fasteners known as 'Velcro'. Hard Velcro is attached to the batten on the wall and soft Velcro to the tapestry itself. This spreads the weight of the panels, whilst still leaving them free-hanging at the bottom edge as they would have done in Henry's time.

Each tapestry is extraordinarily heavy due to the materials, the linings and the gold and silver thread incorporated into them. They are estimated to weigh 10kg per square metre: to hang them today as they would have been in the sixteenth century (with hooks at the top or even by nailing them to the wall) would cause these old weavings to pull themselves apart.

During a spell of wet weather tapestries 'shrink' and 'grow' according to the humidity. Their wool and silk composition will absorb dampness and as the fibres become heavier so the tapestry will lengthen. In drier weather they will return to shape and this has been a continuous process, for the past five centuries or more, without damage to their fabric.

The worth placed on tapestries in the recent past has been overshadowed by the fine arts and the supremacy of Italian artists over northern ones. Tapestries have been valued for their design as though they were paintings without taking account of the weaving skills involved. But 100 years after Henry's death, following the English Civil War, the Abraham tapestries were valued highly by parliament at £8,260 – a far greater sum than for any other work of art in the royal collection. Cardinal Mazarin, Chief Minister of Louis XIV of France, wanted to purchase the set, but ultimately the Commonwealth government did not sell them. Oliver Cromwell kept them for his own use, as Lord Protector, realising the worth of these magnificent weavings.

Panels from the Abraham set were hung in Westminster Abbey for the coronations of Elizabeth I in 1559 and James II in 1685. It is telling that when William III became king in 1689, he did not commission a new set of tapestries for his apartments at Hampton Court but employed these hangings, woven 150 years earlier. It is no exaggeration to say that the magnificent Abrahams, an emblem of the power and splendour of the Tudor dynasty, comprise today the richest and most splendid set of tapestries anywhere in the world to have survived from this period.

8

PAINTING A DYNASTY: THE FAMILY OF HENRY VIII

LITTLE ONE, EMULATE THY FATHER AND BE THE HEIR OF HIS VIRTUE; THE WORLD CONTAINS NOTHING GREATER

INSCRIPTION FROM *EDWARD VI AS A CHILD* BY HANS HOLBEIN THE YOUNGER

HANS HOLBEIN DIED IN 1543, depriving Henry VIII's court of its greatest artistic genius. Two years later, Holbein's likeness of the king was replicated in an anonymous painting entitled *The Family of Henry VIII*, but here the younger, defiant Henry of the Whitehall Mural has been replaced with an older monarch, presiding over his dynasty and striving to secure its future. The composition seems to have been conceived as a sequel to the earlier wall painting.

The Family of Henry VIII

English/Flemish school, c. 1545, oil on canvas, Royal Collection Trust

This portrait of the king and his family shows him seated in the centre of the canvas beneath a canopy of estate. He is flanked on one side by his third wife, Jane Seymour, and on the other by Prince Edward. To the left is the Lady Mary, Henry's daughter by Katherine of Aragon, and on the right the Lady Elizabeth, his daughter by Anne Boleyn. The third Act of Succession of Henry VIII's reign had been passed by Parliament in July 1543, restoring both Mary and Elizabeth to the line of the succession behind their half-brother Edward. It is likely that by this point in time the ageing king had given up hope of fathering another son.

The picture plane is divided into three sections by decorated stone columns. Henry, Jane and their son Edward are enclosed in the central space: a place of authority and legitimacy. Only this immediate royal family are positioned under the canopy of state and standing on the carpet. The two daughters are relegated to the outer sections of the painting – along with jesters or fools – because their future was less assured. Declared illegitimate by an Act of Parliament in 1536, they have been distanced from the symbols of monarchy. Elizabeth lost her status as a result of her mother's fall from favour and Mary had finally capitulated to her father's demands, acknowledging his ecclesiastical supremacy and her own bastardy. The composition calls to mind an altarpiece – a triptych – with the princesses in the position usually reserved for saints and angels, while Henry VIII, Jane Seymour and the young Edward occupy the space traditionally reserved for the Holy Family.

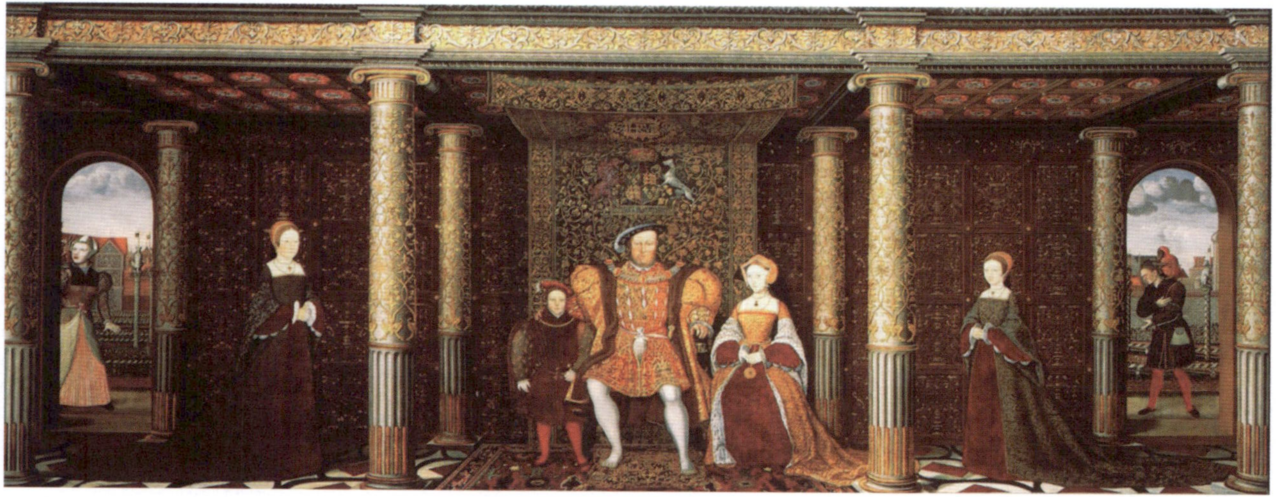

A family portrait, probably painted for Henry VIII and first displayed in the Presence Chamber at Whitehall Palace.

The king is portrayed around the age of 54 and approaching the end of his life. Although the artist shows Henry's legs as still shapely, in reality they were bandaged to cover offensive-smelling abscesses. His feet can be seen, positioned on a plump brocade cushion, encased in square-toed fashionable shoes of the most expensive kind, covered in satin. While the facial likeness of Henry is conceivably fairly accurate, the unknown artist is primarily aiming to convey the king's magnificence, his healthy heir, and the prestige of the Tudor dynasty. In Henry's sixth wife, his children found an excellent stepmother who worked hard to reconcile the king with his daughters and who was very much alive in 1545, when she was omitted from the family painting. By modern standards it may seem insensitive on Henry's part to replace his present queen's likeness with that of his previous wife Jane Seymour, but Jane was the heir's mother and therefore it was essential that she was portrayed. It was of prodigious importance to the survival of the Tudor dynasty that the family of Henry VIII was perceived as strong, stable and united, with a healthy, male heir. Queen Jane is commemorated as the mother not just of Edward but of the future Tudor dynasty.

CLOTHING

Henry VIII used his wardrobe, and that of his family and household, as a way of expressing his wealth and magnificence. The gowns shown in *The Family of Henry VIII* were created using luxurious fabrics, and the jewels are significant. Henry's fur-lined gown hides much of his considerable bulk of around 30 stone. The king's weight increased through the 1540s and male fashion became bulkier, emulating his broad-shouldered image. In an effort to copy the king's physique, some even resorted to padding their doublets. As in the Whitehall Mural, here is Henry at the forefront of European fashion. The king was the nation, and the magnificence of his wardrobe symbolised the wealth of England in the world at large. Dress was an excellent vehicle for the expression of splendour because of the rarity of expensive and sumptuous garments. Few members of the elite could rival the monarch, and only slightly down the social scale access to silk and furs was limited. Sumptuary laws dictated what colour and type of clothing, furs, fabrics and trims were allowed to persons of various ranks or incomes. In the case of clothing, this was intended to reduce spending on foreign textiles, to protect the English wool trade and to ensure that people did not dress above their rank. Such legislation was not new by the sixteenth century but the Tudors passed more Acts against the wearing of costly apparel than any other dynasty. Henry's very first Act of Parliament, in 1509, contained detailed sumptuary laws, confining certain fabrics and colours, such as purple, to the royal family. The king's wardrobe contained a riot of vivid, strong colour, which would make him stand out and emphasise his wealth. Wardrobe warrants included orders for doublets and gowns in yellow, white, orange, carnation and black – which happened to be an extremely expensive dye. The nobility had to tread a careful path, ensuring that they dressed appropriately while not being seen to usurp the king's opulent dress. In 1521, when the Duke of Buckingham was tried for treason, he was also charged with using expensive clothes as a way of drawing support away from the king. At the trial of Anne Boleyn, she was accused, along with her brother George, of having laughed at something the king was wearing. The inclusion of such charges may seem strange to modern observers, but the Tudors took clothing seriously.

Anne's successor, Jane Seymour, was queen for less than eighteen months, so there were few portraits of her. The anonymous artist of this painting appears to have copied her facial likeness from the Holbein portrait that is today in the Kunsthistorisches Museum. Her clothes, too, date from seven or eight years earlier. But the quality of the Vienna portrait far exceeds that of Jane's portrait in *The Family of Henry VIII*.

The princesses Mary and Elizabeth both wear French hoods and are dressed alike, whereas Jane Seymour is wearing an English gabled hood that was still fashionable in her lifetime and in which Holbein painted her. French hoods allow some of the hair to be seen, whereas English hoods cover it completely. Their gowns are of coloured damask, with skirts mounted over Spanish farthingales. Damask is a fabric that uses different weaving techniques to create a variety of elaborate patterns that are always reversible. The sleeves on Mary's gown are a particularly splendid example. Under their skirts, the Spanish farthingales are circular pads of fabric worn around the hips to shape and spread the skirt to enhance the body shape and to display the expensive and intricate fabric. Their exceedingly long trains follow the English fashion and indicate great wealth and status.

Jewellery was an essential part of dressing the elite with gemstones being popular, especially rubies, sapphires and diamonds. The quantity and quality of jewellery was a clear indicator of the sitter's wealth. Jewellery could even be used to demonstrate religious beliefs, classical learning or the family name; the most famous examples are Anne Boleyn's 'A' and 'B' necklaces. Although the half-sisters look very similar in dress, their jewellery is notably individual: Mary wears a cross while Elizabeth has a necklace forming the initial 'A'. Many experts believe this was a jewel that Elizabeth inherited from her mother, Anne Boleyn. It is perhaps surprising that Henry would have permitted such a necklace to be worn as it would have been a reminder of his condemned second wife, and her badges and heraldry were removed from the royal palaces after Anne's execution in 1536. One theory is that the 'A' identifies Elizabeth and highlights her illegitimacy in contrast to the legitimate heir, Edward, standing next to his father. It is also possible that the 'A' was added to the painting during Elizabeth's own reign, in memory of her mother. We know it was hanging in the presence chamber at Whitehall Palace, in 1586–87 when Elizabeth was queen.

THE DYNASTY

After Henry VIII, the most important figure in the painting is Prince Edward, who is around 8 years old and depicted as plump to show that he is in good health. He stands on his father's right, in a place of honour, and the king's hand can be seen on his son's heavily padded shoulder. Edward became the third monarch of the Tudor dynasty and England's first monarch raised as a Protestant. On New Year's Day 1540 Hans Holbein had presented Henry VIII with a superb portrait of Edward wearing a wide-brimmed bonnet and clutching a gold rattle. This important infant who will one day be head of the Church of England raises a tiny hand as if in a blessing. The picture bears the following inscription which, as history would demonstrate, could also apply to Henry's daughters:

> Little one, emulate thy father and be the heir of his virtue; the world contains nothing greater ... Heaven and earth could scarcely produce a son whose glory would surpass that of such a father. Do thou but equal the deeds of thy parent and men can ask no more. Shouldst thou surpass him, thou hast outstript all, nor shall any surpass thee in ages to come.

As king, Edward showed signs of becoming a strong ruler like his father, in a reign characterised by dramatic change and tumult, particularly in terms of religious reformation. But Edward VI did not live long enough to become the great king his father had envisaged: he died of tuberculosis a few months short of his 16th birthday. He regarded his half-sisters Mary and Elizabeth as illegitimate and excluded them from the succession. As his death approached, he changed his will so that his Protestant cousin Jane Grey could inherit the crown, overturning the Third Act of Succession. The traditional view has been that this plot came from the Duke of Northumberland and the regency council, but many historians now see the project as Edward's. He wrote the 'Devise for the Succession' in his own hand.

However, his sister Mary fought for her inheritance to became the first Queen Regnant of England, amid widespread popular support. Her short reign was one of counter-reformation and the burning of Protestants, but she made it possible for women to rule on the same terms as men, setting the stage for her sister Elizabeth to become possibly England's greatest monarch. The great irony in the painting lies in the fact that Henry's true successor stands to his left, outside the pillar of legitimacy: the 11-year-old Elizabeth. Her long reign, from 1558 to 1603, provided peace and stability in

England, allowing the arts to flourish; her moderate stance shaped the Church of England; and the defeat of the Spanish Armada is regarded as one of the most significant military victories in English history.

BACKGROUND

The artist has emphasised the Tudor dynasty by various means: the royal devices and ciphers on the throne canopy declare the substance of Henry's kingship; the Armenian carpet provides evidence of his immense affluence; the gilded pillars, the gold panelling of the walls and the intricate design of the floor are all intentionally ostentatious and sumptuous. The architectural setting appears to depict the interior of Whitehall Palace but we cannot be sure how much is real or imagined. A design for the tapestry *The Healing of the Lame Man* by Raphael has been suggested as a source for the colonnaded location. The Raphael cartoon was one of a set commissioned in 1516 by Pope Leo X for the Sistine Chapel in Rome, widely acknowledged for its influence on art in England. The cartoon can be viewed today in the Victoria and Albert Museum.

The influence of Holbein is evident, not only in the portraiture, but also in the 'antick' style of the architecture and the intricacy of the decorative motifs, which are liberally highlighted in gold. The Tudor roses on the ceiling are of particular significance. They symbolise the end of the Wars of the Roses, the bloody conflict fought between York and Lancaster, the two rival branches of the house of Plantagenet. Having defeated Richard III at Bosworth in 1485, Henry's father, the Lancastrian Henry VII, married Elizabeth of York, uniting the white rose of York and the red rose of Lancaster into arguably the most recognisable emblem in English history. It is a testament to the success of its design that the Tudor rose remains meaningful to the viewer over 500 years after its creation.

FOOLS

The composition of the painting is flat and frieze-like, the only true depth being the view through the archways. Two figures are strikingly framed here. Standing in the archway to the right, with red hose and cropped ginger hair, is Will Somers, court jester to Henry VIII. The monkey on his shoulder (perhaps poised to check his head for lice) is almost certainly a pet belonging to Henry and known as the 'King's Ape'. The woman standing beyond the left archway is probably 'Jane the Fool', who had served Anne Boleyn, Princess Mary and Katherine Parr. The inclusion of fools in this dynastic portrait has been a subject of conjecture. It suggests that they were favoured retainers who held an intimate position within the royal circle. Modern research has found that many court fools were 'natural fools', unconscious of their actions; perhaps people with learning disabilities. In *The Praise of Folly* (published in 1511), the great humanist Erasmus wrote about the wisdom of fools, suggesting that they could be considered holy. He believed they possessed a simple goodness, and that if they were incapable of deliberate sin, they could therefore be conduits of the divine. This may be the reason for the court fools' favour and prominent position in the painting.

Will and Jane, shown wearing high-quality cloth rather than the usual clothing of jesters, were well cared for and valued for their directness and humour. Will Somers was a Shropshire lad who was introduced to the court

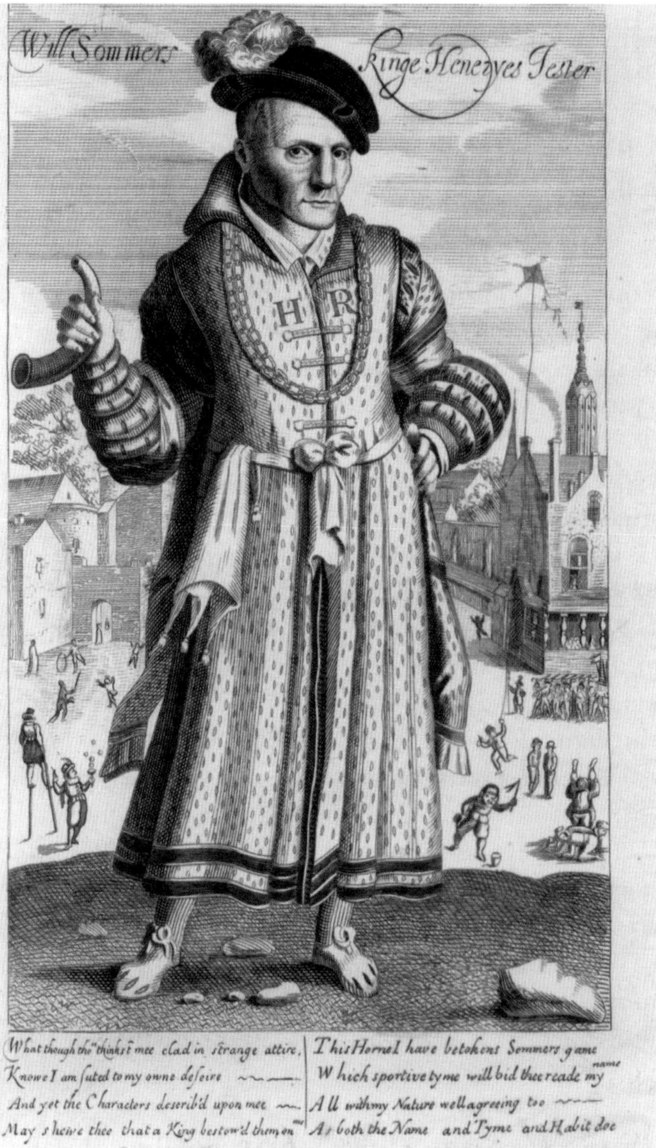

As court jester, Will Somers could lift the king's spirits and sometimes voice uncomfortable truths.

around 1525 and remained in royal service for the rest of his days. When Henry was in pain, or feeling melancholy, Somers was said to be the only person who could lift his spirits. Unlike others in the royal household, Henry's fool was free to voice uncomfortable truths. On some occasions, he was able to jokingly draw the king's attention to abuses within his household. The Elizabethan Privy Councillor, Thomas Wilson, credits Somers with a witty declaration in his *Arte of Rhetorique*. Will is said to have told the king, 'You have so many Frauditors [Auditors], so many Conveighers [Surveyors], and so many Deceivers [Receivers] that they get all to themselves.' Somers appears in other paintings with Henry VIII and his family, including a painting recently discovered at Boughton House, Northamptonshire – testament to the affection in which he was held by the king.

Will Somers remained in royal service for Edward VI and Mary I, dying early in Elizabeth I's reign. The evidence makes a case for his being a natural fool. In 1600, the actor Robert Armin described Somers as 'the king's natural jester' but the most convincing piece of evidence is a warrant from 1551 approving a payment of 40*s* to William Seyton 'whom his Majesty hath appointed to keep William Somer'. This implies that Somers needed a guardian to care for him.

We know that Jane the Fool joined Princess Mary's household after Anne Boleyn's death because Mary's Privy Purse expenses show payments which covered stabling for Jane's horse and expenses for hose, shoes, fabric, and gowns. A few years later, several payments were made to a barber who shaved Jane's head, possibly as the result of a skin disease. She is pictured wearing a close-fitting cap that may be to cover her cropped hair. Jane later joined Katherine Parr's household and there is mention of 'two gowns and two kirtles for Jane the Queen's fool' in a warrant to the Great Wardrobe in June 1546. It is probable that she re-joined Mary's household when Henry VIII died and Edward VI became king. There are recurring entries in Mary's expenses as queen that concern Jane, where she is always referred to as 'Jane our fool'. It appears that Mary looked after her very well, but it is not known what happened to Jane in Elizabeth I's reign. At the time of the family painting in 1545, Jane must have been a familiar figure at court and sufficiently known to be included as the female equivalent to Will Somers.

GARDENS

The scene through the archways behind Will and Jane affords intriguing glimpses of the Privy Garden at Whitehall Palace. Henry VIII took great pleasure in his Privy Gardens, which were accessible from his private lodgings, and he was interested in their planning and construction. In this period, influences from Renaissance Italy were evident in English gardens, typified by a regularity of design combined with architectural features such as banqueting houses on mounts, winding paths, fountains and heraldry. The main rectangle of the garden area was divided into approximately twenty enclosures or 'rooms' defined by wooden posts and rails painted in alternating stripes of white and green. A German visitor during the reign of Elizabeth I described the ground within these enclosures as 'very much resembling a chessboard' with the earth divided up in 'square cavities', some of which were filled with red brick dust, some with white sand, and some with green lawn. In the centre of each 'chessboard' was a brass sundial. Fragrant English flowers and herbs grew around the borders, with lavender, rosemary, violets, strawberries, roses, mint and gillyflowers proving particularly popular. Amid the geometric flower beds can be seen wooden animal sculptures bearing the royal coats of arms. These carved and gilded creatures, known as the King's Beasts, are set upon posts, painted with the continued theme of white and green stripes. Henry VIII is known to have had 180 heraldic animals in his Privy Garden including lions, greyhounds, dragons, panthers, bulls and yales. The King's Beasts are a mixture of mythical and real animals. Among the fictitious creatures was the yale, an animal with the body of an antelope, a lion's tail and horns that could swivel in any direction to protect itself from attack. The yale was originally included in the coat of arms of Henry's grandmother, Margaret Beaufort. A greyhound is pictured in each doorway both to left and to right. It is a Lancastrian emblem and a Tudor one. Henry adopted the breed for his personal standard in 1513 and it appears as a Royal Supporter on the Royal Arms of England. In its time, it would have served as a reminder of the extent of the Tudor dynasty.

Through the left archway can be seen part of the palace, perhaps Princess Mary's lodgings, painted externally with grotesques. Grotesques are distorted fanciful forms that take their name from the Italian *grotteschi*, decorations discovered *c.* 1500 during excavation of ancient Roman houses. They remained a popular form of furniture and interior design throughout the seventeenth century. The view through the right archway is of the north transept of Westminster Abbey and a single turret of Henry VIII's Great Close Tennis Court. Whitehall Palace was destroyed by fire in 1698, and so these details are of great historical interest and importance.

ENGLISH PAINTING

Frustrating as it is not to know the artist of this work, it was common for a sixteenth-century picture not to bear the mark of its creator. Early Tudor portraits were mostly unsigned because the English painter held little status. To the Tudor mind, it was the patron who was considered most worthy of mention, not the artist who created it.

Without a signature, paintings can only be grouped together by artistic style. The label 'English school' is seen frequently in galleries; awarded with hindsight and on visual assessment to portraits that share common features. In the early part of Henry's reign, some of the artistic characteristics that émigré painters brought with them influenced native English artists. The Netherlandish influence was the most prominent and it can usually be observed only as details in certain parts of a painting that otherwise can be attributed to an English hand. The pigments and colours used for this picture could be purchased as easily in London as in Northern Europe. Some pigments were produced in England, for example, earth pigments like red ochre, which was even exported. There was a flourishing lead industry in England that could have produced lead white, red lead and verdigris, but the preference appears to have been for verdigris imported from Montpellier near the south coast of France. It may have been that European pigments were of a superior quality and possibly a lower cost to those produced in England: vermillion, for example, had been known in England since the ninth century and yet the pigment supplied in London came mostly from Antwerp. Expensive minerals producing blue and crimson lakes were probably sold by separate specialist dealers because of the financial outlay involved. In London in 1532, for example, a quart of linseed oil was *6d* and a pound of verdigris was 1*s* but a pound of red lake was vastly more expensive at 13*s* 4*d*. Some London-based artists manufactured their own pigments: the English artist Andrew Wright produced a 'pink' by the barrelful that was sold wholesale or retail.

The same pigments that were used by artists were also employed in the pharmacy trade and so, for import purposes, the sale of pigments was generally placed in the category of herbs and spices. The Grocers Company imported pigments into the port of London and they were sold by either the grocers or the apothecaries. The grocers appear to have supplied a larger range of lesser-quality pigments whereas the apothecaries sold higher-quality goods. Outside London a range of pigments may have been available to provincial artists at local fairs. Most resins and gums for use in the production of paintings would have been imported, but pine resin could have been produced within the British Isles. Glue was made from animal skins and therefore easily obtained locally. Brushes were generally produced from weasel or squirrel tails pushed into the quills of feathers of various sizes; larger and stiffer brushes were made from hog's hair. In Italy, olive oil was often used to clean brushes because it was locally produced, reasonably priced and did not dry. The methods used by English artists remains a mystery, though it is known that a different brush was used for each colour.

Surviving wills confirm that London painters were buying and grinding their own pigments. Harry Blankstone, a painter who died in 1540, left some already ground colours to his son-in-law-to-be. Grinding stones, the tool needed to break down and mix the pigments, were bequeathed in a similar fashion. So it is most likely the same pigments were available both in London and on the Continent, but it does not necessarily follow that English artists in this period had the same understanding of how to use them as their European counterparts.

This painting was produced around 1545 and has been expertly cared for by the conservators of the Royal Collection Trust, but after five centuries, even with specialist care and attention, it can be expected that the picture we see today will have altered from that viewed by Henry VIII. In sixteenth-century paintings pigments may darken or fade, paint flakes, thins or becomes opaque and old varnish can darken and distort colours. In the past, the adoption of harsh cleaning methods has been responsible for removing more than intended, erasing some of the artist's original work, but twenty-first-century technology can unlock some of a painting's remarkable secrets. Using infrared reflectography the layers beneath the paint surface become visible and we can see changes that the artist, for one reason or another, made to the original design. Microscopic examination uncovers the artist's brushstrokes and how they handled paint. It reveals how paint layers and glazes were constructed. Colours change through time and pigment analysis can help with dating a painting. It is possible to tell, for example, if the age of the pigments is consistent with the age of the painting. A pigment not introduced until a later age would be inconsistent with a sixteenth-century Tudor painting. X-rays will see through the paint to reveal the structure of the panel underneath. It will allow us to see how it was constructed – and if the picture has been restored in the past, it will usually show up under ultraviolet examination as dark areas. And so today, we probably know more of the Tudor artists' intent than ever before.

9

DEATH AND MEMORIAL: THE BODY OF HENRY VIII

I HAVE BEEN YOUNG AND NOW AM OLD

PSALM 37

28 JANUARY 1547, WHITEHALL PALACE, LONDON

THE ROYAL HOUSEHOLD is hushed in expectation of a death. Seasonal dampness insinuates itself into every corner of the king's residence and in the royal bedchamber a fire is blazing in a desperate attempt to drive away cold and pestilence. Bitter herbs are burnt but their scent does little to cover the stench of a suppurating body. On the mullioned window a frost is forming and obscuring the rapidly whitening outside world to which Henry still belongs.

Almost two hours after midnight the king's last moments are interrupted only by the spitting of wet wood in the fireplace. Reclining on white linen pillows, Henry's eyes are closed. The rich red hue of the embroidered bedcover floats into his consciousness. It is the colour of blood – is it his blood? Or is it the blood of others spilled throughout his tempestuous reign? Only nine days earlier that of his last victim, Henry Howard, Earl of Surrey, stained the scaffold.

In the large and magnificently carved oak bed, Henry's body appears to shrink. A deep sigh leaves him, and the once magnificent body of King Henry VIII becomes a ravaged corpse.

THE KING'S DECLINE AND DEATH

Henry VIII began his kingship in 1509 as a tall, handsome and athletic youth of 17. When his reign ended in 1547, he was an invalid – bloated and overweight. His precise medical history is either now lost or was never documented by his physicians – perhaps for fear of recrimination – but information concerning the king's health can be found in contemporary letters and state papers.

Throughout the early part of his life, Henry enjoyed excellent health. He was strong and robust, took strenuous exercise and indulged in all kinds of vigorous sports and hunting activities. The jousts and tournaments he enjoyed were particularly dangerous and, unsurprisingly, not without incident. He was nearly killed in 1524 while jousting with his friend and brother-in-law Charles Brandon, and the following year he was thrown headfirst into a muddy ditch, where he almost suffocated. In 1527 he sustained an injury to his foot while playing tennis, and in the same year there is mention of an injury to his thigh, possibly a leg ulcer, which later healed.

By 1536 Henry, now in his mid-40s, was overweight. Suits of close-fitting armour provide evidence of a growing waistline. His obesity and other medical problems can be traced to a jousting accident in 1536 in which he suffered another leg wound.

In January, while in a sporting contest at Greenwich, the king fell from his horse and is said to have remained unconscious for two hours. His legs were injured, possibly fractured. The wounds on his limbs initially healed but reappeared shortly afterward, and thereafter ulceration proved to be troublesome. Henry's ulcers were lanced with red-hot pokers to allow them to drain: it was considered dangerous for the king's health if they healed superficially, as it could bring on sepsis and fever. The stench from the ulcers was noted as being significant.

By 1544 Henry found it harder to take exercise and his weight further increased. At 23 years old his armour had been produced with a 35in (89cm) waist and a 42in (107cm) chest. Twenty years later it had increased to a 51in (130cm) waist and a 55in (140cm) chest. His weight is estimated to have been about 30 stone (190kg). After his fall in 1536 the king was plagued by headaches, which soured his mood and led him to fly into sudden rages, during which he became tyrannically unpredictable.

The Imperial envoy, Eustace Chapuys, reported that after his betrayal by Katherine Howard, the king looked old and grey. He had never seen him 'so sad, pensive and sighing'. Henry's state of mind can be gleaned from notes he made in his bibles and devotional books. A verse that he must have found poignant was marked in Psalm 37 – 'I have been young and now am old, yet I have not seen the righteous forsaken.' Henry wrote in the margin *'Dolus dictum'* ('A painful saying').

By 1547 his swollen legs and extreme obesity led to Henry being carried around the Palace of Whitehall in a chair, before finally he took to his bed. The Treasons Act forbade anyone to speak of the king's death but eventually it was Anthony Denny, a member of the privy chamber, who broke the news to Henry that his death was imminent. The day before he died, the king was attended by his confessor, Archbishop Thomas Cranmer, and took Holy Communion. His decline was rapid, and he died at Whitehall Palace on 28 January, at the age of 55.

THEORIES ON THE KING'S HEALTH

The direct cause of Henry VIII's death has been much debated and many papers on the king's medical history have been given at the Royal College of Surgeons. Henry was still a young man when the first ulcer appeared on his thigh and this has led some scholars to consider that it might be evidence of primary syphilis. It was first suggested by the Victorian obstetrician A.S. Currie and it fitted with the moralistic belief of the time that Henry VIII was licentious. Could venereal disease have also caused the miscarriages suffered by Katherine of Aragon and Anne Boleyn? In 1888 Dr Currie published his theory in the *Edinburgh Medical Journal*, and the belief that the king had syphilis became widespread.

Modern experts have doubted that Henry could have thrived for so many years with such an infection. Neither is there compelling evidence that any of his wives, mistresses or children developed the sexually transmitted disease. Furthermore, the 'great pox', as syphilis was known in Tudor times, would have been treated with mercury, but there is no record of Henry's physicians using this remedy and it does not appear in purchase accounts. Nor do any foreign envoys make mention in their dispatches of the king's suffering from this illness, which they undoubtedly would have reported.

Henry's obesity is usually explained by gluttony and leg injuries that prevented exercise, particularly after 1536. At 6ft 2in, he had passed his youth with an athletic build and a slim waist. Family history may also be considered a factor, as modern medical research shows that genetics is a strong determining factor in cases of obesity. Henry looked like his Yorkist grandfather Edward IV, who was also extremely tall and, after an active youth, gained a huge amount of weight and died suddenly at the age of 41. It was noted that he had changed greatly from the healthy young man who first came to the throne, becoming corpulent and sedentary. The chronicler Dominic Mancini recorded: 'in food and drink he was most immoderate: it was his habit, so I have learned, to take an emetic for the delight of gorging his stomach once more.' As Henry VIII became obese, his eyes and mouth appeared smaller in his bloated face, which could be caused by lack of thyroid function or a pituitary abnormality. Such patients often display aggressive behaviour and suffer recurrent headaches, a problem which plagued Henry.

Finally, he may also have suffered a deep vein thrombosis due to his obesity and immobility. His risk of high blood pressure and Type 2 diabetes would also have been elevated. Swollen legs were perhaps representative of congestive heart failure. The king most likely died from a combination of the ailments that plagued him, finally succumbing to a pulmonary embolism, a blood clot in the lung.

Henry VIII in old age

Cornelis Metsys, c. 1548, line engraving, National Portrait Gallery, London

The Flemish artist and engraver Cornelis Metsys produced a line engraving of Henry VIII which shows the old king as grossly overweight and bloated.

Metsys was born in Antwerp around 1510 but was forced to leave his native city in 1544 because of his religious beliefs. The engraving was produced that year, and there has been speculation that the artist was exiled in England. The date 1548 under the royal coat of arms refers to the year it was printed, not the year of its production.

To produce a line engraving, the design is cut into a metal plate and any shading required is produced by cross-hatching. Line engraving originated in the mid-fifteenth century in Italy and Germany and became a way for artists to sell engraved prints of their paintings for the mass market. This portrait is of note because it is the earliest contemporary print of an English monarch in the Royal Collection.

Henry VIII is richly dressed, but this is not otherwise a flattering portrait. The gloves clasped in front of him would at one time have indicated that he was a man of action, but now they send a contradictory message because this is clearly a man no longer capable of physical activity. The king is at the end of his life: his eyes swollen and his nose crooked; under his beard are the jowls of an old man. Henry's face seems to reflect traits we associate with him in old age, for he looks suspicious, corpulent, covetous and cunning. His personality had changed from the enlightened young king of 1509 who wished to rule justly. The streak of tyranny evident during the 1520s

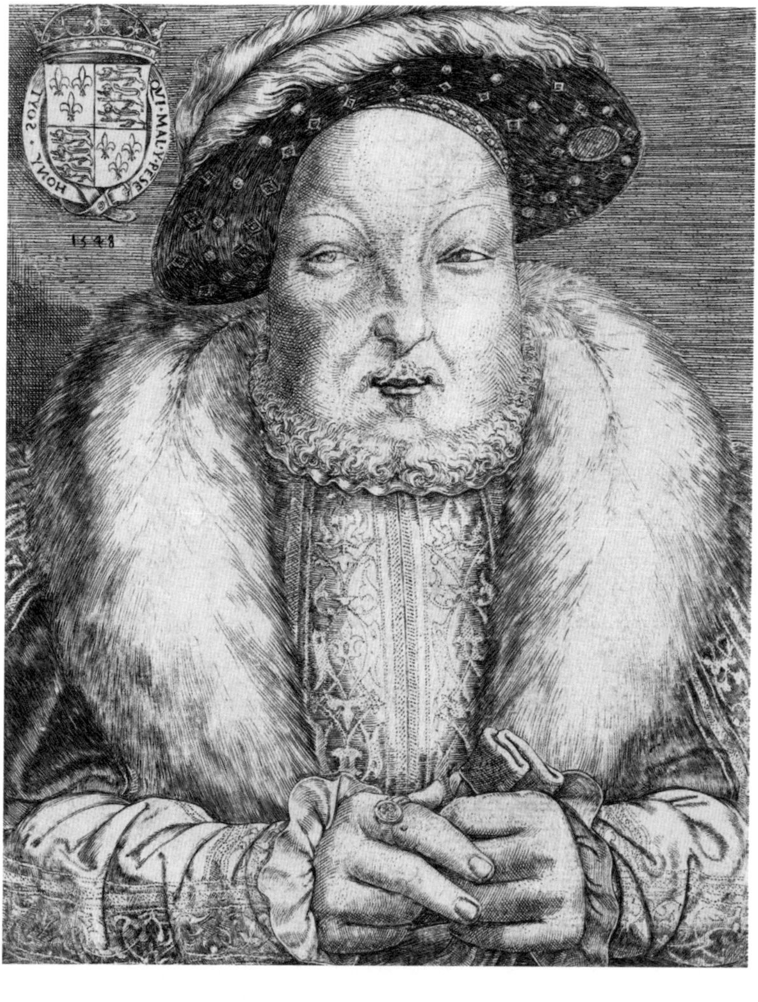

This engraving was produced in 1544 and again in the year following Henry's death.

and 1530s became even more pronounced in the 1540s with high-profile executions such as that of his disgraced Chief Minister, Thomas Cromwell, and Margaret Pole, Countess of Salisbury. Neither posed any real threat to Henry and the latter was a frail old lady who died for her royal blood.

Even so, this late image of Henry VIII is a reminder of his intent to display his magnificence to the very end. Young and old, Henry was a master at wielding royal splendour as a tool of power.

BURIAL

> Our own body be buried and interred in the choir of our College of Windsor, midway between the stalls and the high altar and there to be made and set … an honourable tomb for our bones to rest in, which is well onward and almost made therefore ready with a fair grate about it … in which we will also [that] the bones of our true and loving wife Queen Jane be put also.
>
> Will of Henry VIII, 1546

Church bells tolled throughout the land as Henry's massive body was embalmed and encased in lead. It then lay in state in the presence chamber of Whitehall Palace, surrounded by burning tapers. In Paris, Francis I ordered a Requiem Mass for Henry, but the French king soon followed his old rival to the grave. The two magnificent princes of the Field of the Cloth of Gold died within two months of each other.

On 14 February, the body of Henry VIII began its journey from London to Windsor, in a solemn procession that was

4 miles long. An elaborate hearse bore the vast coffin, which was draped in velvet and cloth of gold, surmounted by a wax effigy. Magnificent to the end, Henry's likeness was clad in crimson velvet, a black satin cap set with precious stones and topped with a crown.

The funeral cortege broke their journey that night at Syon Abbey and arrived at Windsor Castle the following day. Here, sixteen members of Henry's Yeoman Guard – strong and unusually tall, like the king himself – carried his coffin into St George's Chapel. Stephen Gardiner, Bishop of Winchester, conducted a Requiem Mass as Katherine Parr watched from the oriel window originally built for Henry's first wife, Katherine of Aragon. After the ceremony – and according to tradition – the chief officers of the household broke their white staves of office to mark the end of their service. Trumpets sounded as they threw them into the vault where the coffin had been laid.

Thus, Henry VIII became the only Tudor monarch not to lie in Westminster Abbey; he is buried instead at Windsor, unexpectedly away from the tomb of his parents. But the king who grew up enthralled by the romance of medieval chivalry had long chosen this spiritual home of the Knights of the Garter to be his final resting place. He left clear instructions that he wished to join his beloved wife Jane Seymour, who had been buried in St George's after a magnificent funeral in 1537. (He regarded Jane, the mother of his sole legitimate male heir, as the matriarch of his dynasty.)

His choice of Windsor may also have been influenced by the fact that Henry VI was interred there. Henry VII had tried to obtain saintly status for the last Lancastrian king, perhaps as a way of legitimising the new Tudor dynasty, but he was unsuccessful. Henry VIII sustained his father's quest to beatify the Lancastrian king but his divorce and separation from the Church of Rome forced the matter to be abandoned. It is possible that Henry VIII planned to make Windsor a royal mausoleum for all kings. However, this vision was not realised until the early nineteenth century and George III's creation of the Royal Vault. Most kings and queens since George III have been buried at St George's or in the family's private burial ground at Frogmore in the grounds of Windsor Castle.

PLANS FOR A MAGNIFICENT TOMB

The grave of Henry VIII and Jane Seymour was only intended to be a temporary resting place, until a grand monument was completed in another part of the chapel. Unsurprisingly, Henry had planned a magnificent joint tomb, surmounted by effigies of himself and Jane. This tomb would do much more than mark his grave for posterity: it would show all his power, status and wealth. Furthermore, within the Catholic Church, monuments had a religious purpose: to remind worshippers to pray for the soul of the departed, trapped in purgatory. Despite his break with Rome, Henry was still an adherent of such traditional beliefs. For his tomb, he requested 'a convenient altar honourably prepared and apparelled with all manner of things requisite and necessary for daily masses there to be said perpetually while the world shall endure'. Neither the tomb, nor the masses, would be completed as Henry had stipulated.

Tombs were often constructed during the lifetime of those commemorated and so it was for Henry VIII, with his strong desire to demonstrate, in perpetuity, his importance and prestige. In 1519, he had commissioned Pietro Torrigiano to produce a dual monument for himself and his wife of ten years, Katherine of Aragon. It was to be a more magnificent tomb than that of his parents, but Torrigiano departed England before the project was even begun. In 1524, planning his own memorial, Thomas Wolsey had commissioned the great Italian sculptor Benedetto da Rovezzano to construct a monument that was 'not to be inferior in workmanship, magnificence or cost to the tomb of Henry VII'. Rovezzano worked on the tomb for five years, before the Cardinal's fall from grace, when the black marble sarcophagus, pillars and completed statues were immediately appropriated by the king. This included four large bronze angels that were originally intended to stand at the corners of the tomb. In 2015, after a national appeal, they were acquired by the Victoria and Albert Museum. Henry's Chief Minister, Thomas Cromwell, made a number of payments to metal founders during the early 1530s for work on the king's tomb. But Rovezzano was losing his eyesight, caused by the chemical fumes of the metal furnaces used to melt the copper and bronze. He returned to Florence around 1543, but not before an effigy of Henry had been cast and polished.

During the seventeenth century, the antiquarian John Speed unearthed a manuscript from 1527 that gave details of this tomb, for which no expense was to be spared. Entitled *The manner of the Tombe to be made for the Kings Grace at Windsor,* this ostentatious design is in keeping with our perception of Henry VIII and his all-consuming vanity. The plans called for a vast edifice of white marble pillars, gilded bronze angels and life-size images of Henry and his queen. This monument, to one of England's greatest sovereigns, was to be 28ft high, 15ft long and topped by an effigy of the king on horseback, under a triumphal arch. Over 100 brass gilt figures were to adorn the tomb, including St George, St John the

Baptist, the Apostles and the Evangelists. The design also called for an altar at the east end of the tomb, to be enclosed by a black marble and bronze chantry chapel where masses could be said for the king's soul. The monument was intended to surpass not just that of his father, Henry VII, but those of any Pope or monarch to be found in the churches of Europe. In short, it is exactly what we would have expected from Henry VIII.

However, work was extremely slow, perhaps due to costly wars in France and Scotland which drained the royal treasury. The tomb was still unfinished by the time Henry made his will and, although each of his three children expressed their intention to complete the memorial, they failed to do so. This has at times been explained by the lack of skilled artists in England who could complete the project, while others put it down to expense. A further explanation considers that while the Tudor dynasty was in its infancy, tombs and monuments were a crucial element in establishing the royal line, but after Henry died leaving a male heir, the necessity for glorification was less pressing.

The king had left money for prayers to be said for his soul until the end of the world, but the Protestant government of his son stopped the masses after a year. In 1550 they passed The Act of Uniformity, removing religious images from churches. Henry's high-Renaissance tomb design, with its bronze candlesticks, angels and saints, now appeared very Catholic. Edward VI died in 1553, leaving a request in his will that his father's tomb be finished but his sister, Queen Mary I, did not complete the monument. Queen Elizabeth I had some interest in the project and new plans were prepared in 1565. However, work came to a standstill through lack of funds. In 1599, the Swiss physician and traveller Thomas Platter noted in his diary that, 'In the middle of the choir in the said church I saw the grave where Henry VIII had been laid. There is only a rectangular bier on the tomb covered with a miserable tapestry as they have no tomb splendid enough to bury him in.' It seems that not one of Henry's children appeared in a hurry to complete his sepulchre.

A century after Henry's death, the Commonwealth Parliament sold his effigy to be melted down, and in 1649 his tomb was opened to receive the coffin of the executed Charles I. Just before the close of the seventeenth century, another tiny coffin was laid on top of King Charles's: one of the many dead infants of his granddaughter, Queen Anne. In 1805, the black marble sarcophagus that had been Wolsey's and Henry's was taken to the crypt of St Paul's Cathedral and used for Admiral Lord Nelson's monument, where it can still be seen today.

EXCAVATION OF THE ROYAL VAULT

In 1813, excavation commenced for a passage to a new royal vault and the old vault was opened in the presence of the Regent, George Prince of Wales, and his physician, Sir Henry Halford, who recorded:

> Neither of the other coffins had any inscription upon them. The larger one, supposed on good grounds to contain the remains of King Henry VIII, measured six feet ten inches in length, and had been inclosed [*sic*] in an elm one of two inches in thickness: but this was decayed, and lay in small fragments near it. The leaden coffin appeared to have been beaten in by violence about the middle; and a considerable opening in that part of it exposed a mere skeleton of the

> king. Some beard remained upon the chin, but there was nothing to discriminate the personage contained in it. The smaller coffin, understood to be that of Queen Jane Seymour, was not touched; mere curiosity not being considered, by the Prince Regent, as a sufficient motive for disturbing these remains.

The Prince Regent requested a marble slab be inserted to mark the grave but this didn't materialise until the reign of his successor. The inscription on the memorial reads: 'In a vault beneath this marble slab are deposited the remains of Jane Seymour Queen of King Henry VIII 1537, King Henry VIII 1547, King Charles I 1648 and an infant child of Queen Anne. This memorial was placed here by command of King William IV. 1837.'

So, in stark contrast to his life, Henry's grave is identified by a simple, plain black tile, engraved with gold lettering, while his contemporary, King Francis I, reposes in splendour, in the Basilica of St Denis in Paris. There can be little doubt as to what Henry's reaction would be to his fate.

Sketch of Henry VIII's vault

Alfred Young Nutt, Royal Collection Trust

During the reign of Queen Victoria, in 1888, the royal vault was opened once more, when it was decided that some relics taken from the coffin of Charles I in 1813 should be returned. Alfred Young Nutt, an English architect and artist who was Surveyor to the Dean and Canons of St George's Chapel, made a sketch of the vault at this time. Nutt recorded that Henry's coffin was about 2m in length and

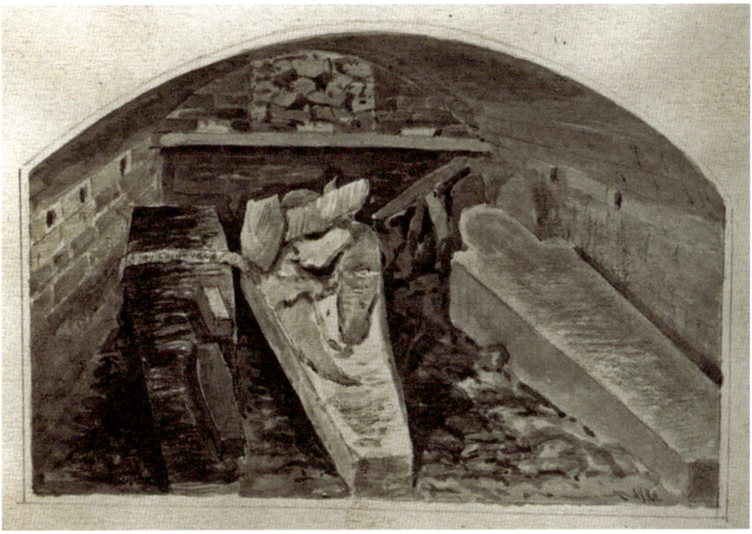

Sketch of Henry VIII's Vault by Alfred Young Nutt, 1888.
King Henry VIII (centre, damaged), Queen Jane (right),
King Charles I (left).

was in a state of disrepair with some bodily remains visible. Nutt's sketch shows that Henry VIII's coffin has been damaged. This could have happened by accident during the internment of Charles I or the trestle supporting the heavy coffin may have collapsed at some point.

There is a macabre story that Henry's coffin burst, oozing liquids, as his body spent the night at Syon, and that a dog had licked his blood. This was thought to fulfil a prophecy made by the Franciscan friar William Peto, who had denounced the king's divorce in 1535, saying that 'God's judgements were ready to fall upon his head and that dogs would lick his blood, as they had done to Ahab'. The tale of coffin-leaking was taken up by Bishop Gilbert Burnet in the late seventeenth century. In his *History of the Reformation* he stated that this happened to Henry's body at Syon. Agnes Strickland later embellished the story when she wrote *The Lives of the Queens of England* in the nineteenth century.

> A most invincible King, whose acquirements and qualities are so many and excellent that I consider him to excel all who ever wore a crown.
>
> Francesco Chieregato,
> Apostolic Nuncio in England, 1517

Henry VIII was a complex and contradictory man. The handsome, intelligent and charming Renaissance prince who became a ruthless and cruel tyrant. He was a natural conservative, but he introduced radical change by breaking with the Church of Rome and founding the Church of England. He married six times and lamented that such a kind and gentle husband (or so he thought) had been disappointed by many 'ill-conditioned' wives. Henry never lost sight of himself as a noble knight, inspired by childhood stories of chivalry. He pursued a foreign policy of aggression towards France and Scotland that drained the royal coffers, without lasting benefits. But Henry VIII has also been called 'the father of the English Navy' and his increased fortifications secured England's shores against invasion. In 1536 the Act of Union united Wales with England and in 1541 Henry was accorded the title King of Ireland. During his reign the power of the nobles diminished and that of Parliament increased, particularly over matters of taxation. It is reasonable to consider that Henry VIII changed his country for the generations to come and that he laid the foundation for a modern Britain.

It is ironic that a king who embodied magnificence and lived so opulently should lie in a plain vault, marked only by a marble slab. The father with whom he competed still rests in the glorious Renaissance tomb his son commissioned in Westminster Abbey.

10

THE ROYAL COLLECTION: HENRY VIII AND AFTERWARDS

THROUGHOUT ALL MY LIFE AND WITH ALL MY HEART I SHALL STRIVE TO BE WORTHY OF YOUR TRUST

QUEEN ELIZABETH II

HENRY VIII AND THE ROYAL COLLECTION

HENRY VIII'S RELATIONSHIP with the King of France was one of continued rivalry, but as someone who prized beautiful and valuable things, Henry admired and wanted to emulate Francis I's magnificent royal collection.

Henry patronised artists, musicians and poets, bringing Renaissance values from Italy and France to the English royal court. He assembled all manner of objects on both a grand and a personal scale. In short, it was Henry VIII who laid the foundations of a collection that survives to this day as the Royal Collection.

Following Henry's death in 1547, an inventory was compiled of all his moveable goods and the contents of his many homes. It took more than eighteen months to compile and included thousands of objects, described as 'stuff'. The king stored his 'stuff' within his fifty-five palaces, in the jewel house in the Tower of London and in the Great Wardrobe, the department of the royal household that supplied the king with clothing and furnishings.

The first group of items listed in the inventory is the royal regalia for the king and the queen, including *'The Kinges Crowne of golde'*. The gold and jewels weighed an impressive 278.5oz. The royal regalia was only a small proportion of the precious plate owned by Henry, but it was considered the most important part of the king's collection, not for its weight or its value but for its immense social and religious significance.

The additional 2,028 pieces of plate listed in the inventory were employed to display the king's wealth to his dinner guests or to be used during the celebration of mass. A large proportion of Henry's plate was of contemporary Renaissance design and it provided a visual reminder of both his wealth and his princely good taste.

Only four items from Henry's jewel house survive but they give an idea of the absolute magnificence of Henry's collection. One is the Royal Gold Cup, now in the British Museum in London. Manufactured from solid gold and embellished with enamel and pearls, it stands 236mm high and was created in France at the end of the fourteenth century. It first appears in the records of Henry VIII in 1521 and the Tudor roses on the decoration date to this time. Thomas Hoving, former director of the Metropolitan Museum in New York, commented that 'of all the princely jewels and gold that have come down to us – this is the most spectacular – and that includes the great royal treasures.'

Another survivor from Henry VIII's collection is a gold clock salt cellar adorned with cameos, now owned by the Worshipful Company of Goldsmiths in London. It was made in Paris, *c.* 1530, by Pierre Mangot, goldsmith to Francis I. How it came to be part of Henry VIII's collection is unknown, but possibly it was an impressive diplomatic gift from the French king.

Two more items can be seen today: a London-made rock crystal and silver-gilt cup survives in the Treasury of San Lorenzo in Florence and a gold and enamelled rock crystal bowl, set with diamonds, rubies, emeralds and pearls is in the collection of the Schatzkammer of the Residenz in Munich.

The designs by Hans Holbein for a cup for Jane Seymour are conserved at the Ashmolean Museum in Oxford. The cup was fabricated, and it featured in the inventories of royal plate, but it was melted down in the seventeenth century – the sad fate of so many of Henry's treasures.

The king's elaborate clothes were embellished with pure gold ornaments that were detachable and recycled from one gown to another. After his funeral, the precious metal was collected and recorded at Whitehall as 1,510.5oz of 'ingoldes of silver conteyening gold coming of the Kinges burul apparal'.

Henry acquired an extensive collection of personal jewellery. Around twenty coffers contained items that Henry wanted close at hand wherever he went. Not all the items in the coffers were as monetarily precious as his jewels; they included private necessities such as bandages for his legs or his favourite books. The library at Whitehall Palace contained 1,450 books, a further 329 resided at Greenwich and more were preserved within his many palaces. His books and manuscripts have survived surprisingly intact and a selection can be viewed in the British

Library in London. Henry accumulated manuscripts and, according to the British Library, around 20 per cent of the old royal manuscript holdings entered the collection under Henry VIII – more than can be associated with any other monarch.

Besides keeping hawks and falcons – and nightingales hung in cages – the king had a fondness for dogs. He kept beagles and spaniels, but his favourite breed of dog was the greyhound. They were considered an especially noble breed, and the greyhound was a symbol of the Earldom of Richmond, a title held by Henry VII. Henry gave gifts of dogs to Francis I and to the Holy Roman Emperor. The king's dogs wore white silk coats and richly decorated velvet collars, and sixty-five dog leashes were included in the 1547 inventory.

A bizarre description of a set of wooden chessmen is noted, of which four were broken. A curious item, previously considered to have been part of a costume for masques, is now in the Victoria and Albert in London, where it is described as an item of personal hygiene: an impressive solid gold toothpick and earpick.

The king's wardrobe of clothes included forty-one gowns, twenty-five pairs of hose and forty girdles (belts). He possessed eight walking staves and among his personal armoury were ninety-four swords and thirty-six daggers. Decorative certainly, but also a sign of the turbulent times in which he lived. Either from sentimentality or the fact that they were simply forgotten, there remained in Henry's collection his brother Arthur's garter robes and the clothes of his third queen, Jane Seymour, who had died in 1537.

Animal furs including ermine, lynx, sable, leopard and squirrel were employed to enrich Henry's gowns and those of his courtiers, with sable being a favourite.

In 1543/44, Henry paid £166 for eighty sables for a gown of damask. Also catalogued was a collection of brightly coloured feathers to adorn his hats and bonnets.

Whitehall Palace held a stockpile of fabrics with an estimated worth of over £50,000, including cloth of gold, silk, embroidered damask, and velvet. For comparison, the annual income of a duke was about £6,000 per annum and a commoner's wage amounted to around 2½*d* per day. Luxury textiles like these were highly prized and costly, requiring great expertise to create and usually made only in small quantities. After Henry's death an incredible 8,000 yards of silk lay in the silk house at Whitehall.

From a huge collection of 2,450 tapestries and wall hangings, just over 100 survive, with twenty-eight of them in the Royal Collection. The Abraham tapestries still hang in all their glory in the Great Hall at Hampton Court Palace, the site for which they were designed and from where they continue to attract as much admiration as they did during the reign of Henry VIII. In 1659, thirteen fragments of tapestry borders from the collection of Henry VIII and Cardinal Wolsey were recorded as hanging in the 'withdrawing room' and from 1849 a selection of these armorial tapestry fragments have been hanging at Hampton Court Palace, alongside the Abraham Tapestries.

Tudor carpets exemplified much more than a means of providing warmth and decoration; they were a luxury that only the wealthy could afford and represented high status. In private homes, they were hung on a wall or displayed on a table for guests to admire. In important rooms in the royal palaces they were spread on the floor, often over rush matting. Full-length portraits of Henry VIII often depict him standing on a carpet, an allusion to wealth and privilege that would not have been overlooked by the contemporary viewer. Within the palace, carpets were classified according to their function, for example, foot carpets, carpet cushions or table carpets. Henry's collection was principally Turkish and of decorative Chintamani and Ushak design. More than 800 carpets are listed in the inventory – 200 of them at Hampton Court Palace.

Henry VIII and other members of his court, including the courtier Sir Nicholas Poyntz, appreciated fine glass, principally Venetian. In 1540, Henry bought large quantities of glass that was cared for by James Rufforthe in the old jewel house at Westminster. Glass items were not as valuable as other categories in the collection, but they were exhibited around the palaces in small groups, admired and conversed over for their unique and fragile beauty. The king's glass house at Whitehall contained 774 pieces.

In the sixteenth century, 'true' hard paste porcelain manufactured in China was considered highly exotic and extremely valuable. It was listed in the 1547 inventory as 'purselyn' and Henry was the first English sovereign known to have owned such a rarity.

Playing music and composing was a favourite diversion for the king, who was also an enthusiastic patron of musicians. Music played an indispensable part of every aspect of court life, from baptisms, coronations and funerals to pageants and court masques. Henry appointed Philip van Wilder, a Franco-Flemish musician and lute player, Keeper of the King's Instruments. Included in the 1547 inventory were twenty recorders, nineteen viols, two clavichords and four sets of bagpipes – including one made of purple velvet.

Henry VIII was in a position to indulge in all kinds of collecting activities and he owned a very large number of paintings and sculptures, many of the latter in terracotta. The whole collection was spread about the various royal palaces, with Whitehall housing a large number of pictures. The works were beautifully framed, with wood that was painted and gilded, and they were usually protected by curtains drawn over them. The king would order the hangings to be opened when he wished to look at the paintings.

The Family of Henry VIII was probably painted for Henry and has remained in the Royal Collection to the present day. In addition to offering the viewer a portrait of the royal family, it depicts the first recognisable garden in British art. In 2015, the painting appeared in the exhibition *Painting Paradise: The Art of the Garden* at the Queen's Gallery in Buckingham Palace, where it was of great interest to horticulturalists and garden historians, a reminder that a painting can often reveal more than the primary subject matter.

The Field of the Cloth of Gold has also remained in the Royal Collection. It has been noticeably damaged, and it is obvious that the head of Henry VIII has been cut from the canvas at some point. Without documentation to explain why this should have happened, a romantic story has been perpetuated: to prevent the painting from being sold during the Civil War, a cavalier removed Henry's head with his sword and pocketed it, making the picture unsaleable. After the restoration, it is said that the head was restored, and the painting once again took its place on the walls of the old Tudor palace.

This painting featured in an eight-part BBC Radio 4 series, *The Art of Monarchy*, to mark Queen Elizabeth II's Diamond Jubilee. The broadcast served to illuminate the long history of British kings and queens through the works of art they acquired, and *The Field of the Cloth of Gold* represented the reign of Henry VIII.

A Protestant Allegory, painted for Henry VIII at the time of his break with the Church of Rome, appeared in the same programme to illustrate the complex religious history of the second Tudor king. Over the 500 years and more since Henry's reign, some of his paintings have had complicated histories and this picture is a good example. *A Protestant Allegory* left the Royal Collection in 1547, and was owned by Henry Fitzalan, 12th Earl of Arundel. He bequeathed it to John, Lord Lumley who returned the painting to the Royal Collection of Charles I. The king exchanged it with Philip Herbert, 4th Earl of Pembroke who, in turn, gave it to Thomas Howard, 14th Earl of Arundel. In 1675, it was purchased from Arundel by Charles II and – finally– it ended its travels by becoming part of the Royal Collection once again.

The Battle of the Spurs did not appear in either the 1542 or the 1547 inventory of Henry's goods because it was most probably set into the walls of Whitehall Palace.

The 150 painted panels in Henry's possession were not considered especially valuable when compared with tapestries and plate, but paintings were a useful vehicle for propaganda purposes. In the 1540s Henry commissioned a series of paintings of earlier kings of England, including Henry V and Richard III. Their likenesses were primitive because they were taken from those found on coins, medals, and seals but it was not their physical attributes that mattered to Henry, it was their status as monarchs of England. They stood for a continuity of royal power that linked Henry with the medieval past; he was inventing a history and a solidity for himself and the relatively new Tudor dynasty. There were also a great many portraits of contemporary European rulers and their families, and there can be no doubt that the fashion for collecting portraits was firmly established by Henry VIII's reign.

We know little about how Henry VIII acquired his collection of pictures, although his accounts record the payment of enormous sums for tapestries made for him in the Low Countries. By the 1530s pictures seem to have been popular as New Year gifts, and others, particularly portraits, must have been gifts from foreign courts. We do know how Henry VIII obtained one picture listed in his collection, the portrait of Christina of Denmark, which is now in the National Gallery, London. As discussed in chapter five, when Henry began his search for a fourth wife, Hans Holbein was sent abroad to portray prospective candidates. When he returned with the likeness of Christina, Henry was said to be enchanted with the result. The Imperial Ambassador Eustace Chapuys noted, 'since he saw it he has been in much better humour than he ever was, making musicians play on their instruments all day long.' The lady herself was reluctant and Henry later married Anne of Cleves, but he kept the portrait of Christina in his collection until his death. Of Henry's consorts, only portraits of Jane Seymour are recorded in the collection in the sixteenth century.

Although his purpose was always to enhance his own glory, Henry VIII was the first English king to collect art in the modern sense. By patronising Hans Holbein, he has left us a remarkable visual record of himself and his court. Enough evidence survives to permit us to visualise the splendour of his palaces and to consider this king not only a great collector, but also the founder of the concept of an English Royal Collection. Henry's great legacy, begun more than five centuries ago, continues to flourish into the twenty-first century under the guardianship of Elizabeth II.

THE ROYAL COLLECTION TO THE PRESENT DAY

The Royal Collection of today is one of the last royal collections in Europe to survive intact. With some 7,000 paintings it is the largest private art collection in the world and, including items from the decorative arts, it amounts to more than one million objects. The monarch does not own the Royal Collection but holds it in trust for future kings and queens and for the nation. The collection is displayed in fifteen royal palaces and former residences where the public can view works 'in the settings for which they were originally commissioned or acquired'.

The whole comprises a captivating expression of the personal taste of successive monarchs over a period of more than 500 years. Unlike any national collection, it has had no obligation to educate or to explain its acquisitions. Being privy to the private selection of each monarch allows the viewer an intimate insight into their various interests and personalities. Some monarchs have taken greater interest in expanding and caring for the collection than others. George I, for example, took little interest in the treasures he inherited, and William IV believed that art was 'for women and imbeciles'. But among the true connoisseurs were King Charles I, King George IV and Queen Victoria – collectors whose taste and enthusiasm greatly expanded and enriched the collection.

From Henry VIII onwards, the collection grew with each successive monarch. By the 1630s, and the reign of Charles I, it rivalled anything similar in Europe. For Charles was not only an informed connoisseur of paintings, he was also a dedicated patron with an educated eye, who supported contemporary artists such as Peter-Paul Rubens and Anthony Van Dyck. Perhaps surprisingly for a passionate art lover, Charles I was indifferent to Holbein. He exchanged Henry VIII's picture of Sir John Godsalve by Holbein with Philip Herbert, 4th Earl of Pembroke. The picture followed the same provenance as *A Protestant Allegory*, with Pembroke giving it to the 14th Earl of Arundel, from whom it was acquired by Charles II. And so, by 1675, the Holbein once again hung in a royal palace.

The collection has witnessed its highs and lows. The English Civil War of the 1640s, and the defeat of the king, had a devastating effect, with St Edward's coronation regalia, which was at the very heart of the monarchy, being melted down at the royal mint to help fund the new Commonwealth government. The only item of the medieval coronation regalia surviving today is a twelfth-century anointing spoon which resides alongside the Crown Jewels at the Tower of London. During the Commonwealth sale, it was sold for £5, hidden safely until the restoration of Charles II in 1660 and then sold back to the monarch for £15 – good return on an investment and a worthy purchase for the Royal Collection. The spoon was last used in 1953 during the coronation ceremony of Elizabeth II.

Following the execution of King Charles in 1649, hundreds of exquisite paintings were sold on the orders of Parliament and many masterpieces left the collection permanently. Some of these works can now be seen in the world's great museums, including the Louvre in Paris. The king's widow, Queen Henrietta Maria, had left England to live in France, transporting with her the Holbein painting known as 'Noli me Tangere', which had graced the walls of Henry VIII's palaces. It was retrieved after her death by her son and is once again the only religious painting by Holbein in the Royal Collection. At present, it is displayed in the Queen's Drawing Room at Windsor Castle.

The monarchy was restored in 1660 when Charles II returned from exile and his subsequent coronation necessitated the remaking of all the coronation regalia. Commissions were placed with Sir Robert Vyner, the royal banker and goldsmith, for the crowning ceremony in April 1661. The diarist Samuel Pepys was present, noting how 'The King came in with his crowne on and his sceptre in his hand – under a canopy borne up by six silver staves, carried by Barons of the Cinqueports – and little bells at every end.' Most of the coronation items presently in the Tower of London date to the reign of Charles II.

The restored king inherited a greatly reduced art collection, although some previously lost paintings were recovered when royal sympathisers returned pieces purchased during the Commonwealth. The set of dynastic portraits, including Henry V and Richard III, that had been commissioned by Henry VIII or his father, was now displayed in the King's Privy Gallery. Unlike his father, Charles II appreciated Holbein and several portraits painted during Henry VIII's reign that had left the collection were repurchased and rehung in the King's Closet. One example was the portrait of Sir Nicholas Poyntz, whose home at Iron Acton in Gloucestershire Henry had visited in August 1535. Poyntz was a stylish lover of fashion and, as mentioned earlier, shared a passion for collecting glass and ceramics with the king.

The States-General of Holland offered gifts of paintings and sculpture to the newly restored king and Charles himself purchased an additional seventy-two paintings. However, prized pieces of the Royal Collection had been lost to Britain forever and absorbed into the collections of the French or Spanish courts.

William and Mary were crowned joint monarchs in 1689, both having a claim to the throne through their shared grandfather Charles I. Mary II had a great passion for oriental porcelain, and it filled her apartments, thus setting a craze among her subjects. Some families were pushed to the brink of bankruptcy for the stylish blue and white china. Mary's collection reflected her own taste but perhaps not so much that of her husband. Following her untimely death from smallpox, William gave away practically her whole collection to his favourite courtier Arnold van Keppel, the Earl of Albemarle. In recent years, pieces of Mary's collection have been traced and repurchased by the Royal Collection Trust, and Mary's oriental porcelain fills her rooms at Kensington Palace and Hampton Court once again.

For all the priceless treasures that enter the Royal Collection there are items that for one reason or another are disastrously lost. In 1698, Henry VIII's Palace of Whitehall was consumed by fire, leaving only the Banqueting House still standing. Lost among the flames was Holbein's Whitehall Mural and a bust of Charles I by Gianlorenzo Bernini, arguably the single greatest loss of any work from the collection.

The early Hanoverian period was not one of great activity for the collection until after the death of George I in 1727, when his daughter-in-law Caroline of Ansbach began to take an interest. Caroline established a personal library at St James's Palace, and it is to her that we owe the pleasure of seeing the lost Holbein drawings from the court of Henry VIII. Incredibly, they had been completely forgotten until Caroline discovered them tucked away in a bureau in Kensington Palace. The album contained around eighty drawings; some were produced during Holbein's first visit to England in 1526–28, but the majority dated to his second stay from 1532, four years before he was appointed as 'King's Painter'. Queen Caroline removed the drawings from the album in around 1730 and had them individually framed, bringing the faces of Henry VIII's courtiers to life once again within the royal palaces in which they had lived and worked. Caroline's love of art was inherited by her estranged son, Frederick, whose taste in paintings was reflected in a passion for French, Flemish and Italian pictures.

George III invested more interest and time in the Royal Collection than any monarch since Charles I. He patronised contemporary artists including Johan Zoffany, Thomas Gainsborough and Benjamin West, and purchased an entire collection of art from Joseph Smith, the British consul in Venice. Such was the king's enthusiasm that he paid £20,000 for the paintings before even seeing them. The collection consisted of priceless drawings and paintings by Giovanni Antonio Canaletto, Marco and Sebastiano Ricci, Giovanni Bellini, and Baldassare Castiglione. Included in a group of Northern European paintings bought by George III was the now well-loved and popular Vermeer picture *Lady at the Virginals*. Almost all the purchases made by George III were used to decorate the walls of Buckingham House (later Palace), which he bought as a private family residence for Queen Charlotte and their growing brood of children. It was George III who acquired the Cornelis Metsys engraving of Henry VIII in old age that dates to *c*. 1548. The picture featured in the exhibition *Henry VIII: A 500th Anniversary Exhibition* at Inner Hall, London, in 2009. The king also acquired rare books from the collection of Joseph Smith in order to fill the shelves of his library and amassed an impressive collection of gems, cameos, coins and medals. In 1823, George IV presented his father's library to the British Museum.

George IV loved to dazzle. He appreciated sparkle and splendour and was possibly the most extravagant of all

British monarchs. The diadem worn by Queen Elizabeth II on British postage stamps was in fact made for George IV to wear en route to his coronation. He was the only British monarch to depart from traditional robes: when he was crowned in 1821 he was heavily influenced by Napoleon's 1804 enthronement in Paris, from the high ruffs reaching to his ears, to his heavily ornate beribboned shoes and ermine-lined train. George was so taken with stylishness that he appears to have overlooked the fact that his own coronation date was set for July, when the heat must have proved unbearable.

Typical of the jewellery admired by George IV is a hat badge with St George and the Dragon, produced by a Flemish artist *c.* 1520, and described in the records as 'an ancient badge Tudor'. Traditionally, it is held as being the 'riche brooch with ye image of saint George' worn by Henry VIII that may have been presented to him by Maximilian. It is an example of the type of jewels that King George acquired from Rundell, Bridge & Rundell, the royal goldsmiths from 1797 to 1840, and it is listed in an inventory of the Royal Collection in 1830 at Windsor Castle.

Just as the French court had purchased Royal Collection works in the aftermath of the English Civil War, George IV was able to acquire high-quality works of art during the disturbance caused by the French Revolution. When the sequestered property of French Royalists became available – at reduced prices – he dispatched his agents to Paris for the specific purpose of making such purchases. He was also able to indulge his love for Dutch and Flemish genre paintings, pictures that depicted ordinary people in everyday situations that were the opposite of his own luxurious lifestyle. George showed little interest in religious paintings or still lifes but he was a patron of George Stubbs, the English painter of horses; the portraitist Thomas Lawrence; and Thomas Gainsborough, who specialised in producing British landscapes but made his living painting portraits.

Queen Victoria expanded the Royal Collection on all levels. Among contemporary artists she supported were David Wilkie, the Scottish genre artist; Edwin Landseer, a painter and sculptor of the famous lions in Trafalgar Square; and particularly Franz Winterhalter, who had the ability to paint Victoria as she wished to be seen, whether it be wife, mother or monarch. On 13 May 1842, she purchased a gilt bronze clock for £110 5*s*. It had an extraordinary history, reputedly being given by Henry VIII to his sweetheart Anne Boleyn on the morning of their marriage in 1532.

In 1849, Victoria bought another Tudor item that would have been of great sentimental value to Henry VIII; a miniature painting by Lucas Horenbout of his illegitimate son by Elizabeth Blount, Henry Fitzroy, Duke of Richmond and Somerset. In desperation at his lack of a son, the king appears to have considered appointing the boy his heir but at the age of 17, Henry Fitzroy died of tuberculosis. The portrait depicts him in casual clothing and is important as, dating from 1533/34, it is one of the first informal portraits in the history of English art. Yet another Tudor work was acquired when the painting of *The Family of Henry VII with St George and the Dragon* came up for sale in 1883 and soon became another addition to the already extensive Royal Collection.

Victoria's consort, Prince Albert, enjoyed early Italian painting, although this was extremely unfashionable at the time. He sent agents abroad to seek out thirteenth- and fourteenth-century works by Giotto of Florence, Duccio of Siena and Fra Angelico, whom Vasari described as 'a rare and perfect talent'. They discovered an altarpiece by Duccio and a painting by Fra Angelico that entered the collection for a spectacularly reasonable £129. Albert's picture choices provided some of the earliest dated examples in the collection and he displayed his paintings principally at Osborne House on the Isle of Wight. After his death, Queen Victoria presented twenty-two of his pictures to the National Gallery in London, in memory of her husband.

It is thanks to Queen Victoria that thousands of visitors began to see treasures of the Royal Collection on display at Hampton Court Palace and at her birthplace of Kensington Palace. Both were opened to the public, free of charge, during the queen's reign. Furthermore, the Gothic Revival, a style which sought to revive medieval forms, reached its height in the nineteenth century, renewing interest in tapestries, stained glass and the decorative architecture of Henry VIII's old buildings.

The contribution of Victoria's son Edward VII reflected his own interests, namely paintings of racehorses, the sea, shooting scenes and portraits of pretty women. Edward VII presented the government of France with a magnificent and generous gift of twelve French fifteenth-century manuscripts as a token of friendship. It was certainly a lavish gift, but one that was more than matched by the government of the Transvaal in 1907. For his 66th birthday they presented Edward VII with the largest diamond ever found, which weighed 3,106.75 carats. It was named the Cullinan Diamond after the chairman of the mine in which it was discovered and was cut into nine large stones and ninety-seven small brilliants. Cullinan I and II are set into the Sovereign's sceptre and Imperial State Crown and are on display in the jewel house in the Tower of London.

George V, grandfather to Queen Elizabeth II, became king in 1910. His interest in the arts was minimal but his wife, Queen Mary, enjoyed collecting pieces of Fabergé, fans, gems, jewels and decorated boxes. In 1924, Queen Mary commissioned the notable architect Sir Edwin Lutyens to design the now famous dollhouse at Windsor Castle. Everything it contained was an exact miniature copy, made by the finest artists, craftsmen and manufacturers. Furniture, pictures, books, bedlinen, kitchen utensils, motor cars and bottles of wine – all were faithfully reproduced to furnish a fascinating record of life as the queen would have known it in the second decade of the twentieth century. There was even a tiny copy of a Holbein portrait of Henry VIII and a miniature Chelsea porcelain figure of the Tudor king.

Queen Elizabeth, the Queen Mother, had an accomplished eye for twentieth-century art. She acquired paintings by British landscape painter and portraitist William Nicholson; the Welsh artist Augustus John; Walter Sickert, a member of the Camden Town group; the war artist Paul Nash; Duncan Grant of the Bloomsbury circle; Graham Sutherland, who designed the tapestry for the rebuilt Coventry Cathedral; and John Piper, a painter and stained-glass maker. She also purchased a painting by Edouard Monet.

Her Majesty Queen Elizabeth II

Unknown artist, c. *1953 wearing the 1820 diadem*

A new openness in displaying the Royal Collection began a year after Elizabeth II came to the throne in 1953, when Her Majesty allowed the public to visit the private rooms of Queen Victoria at Osbourne House. Almost all of her unoccupied royal palaces followed suit, and there has

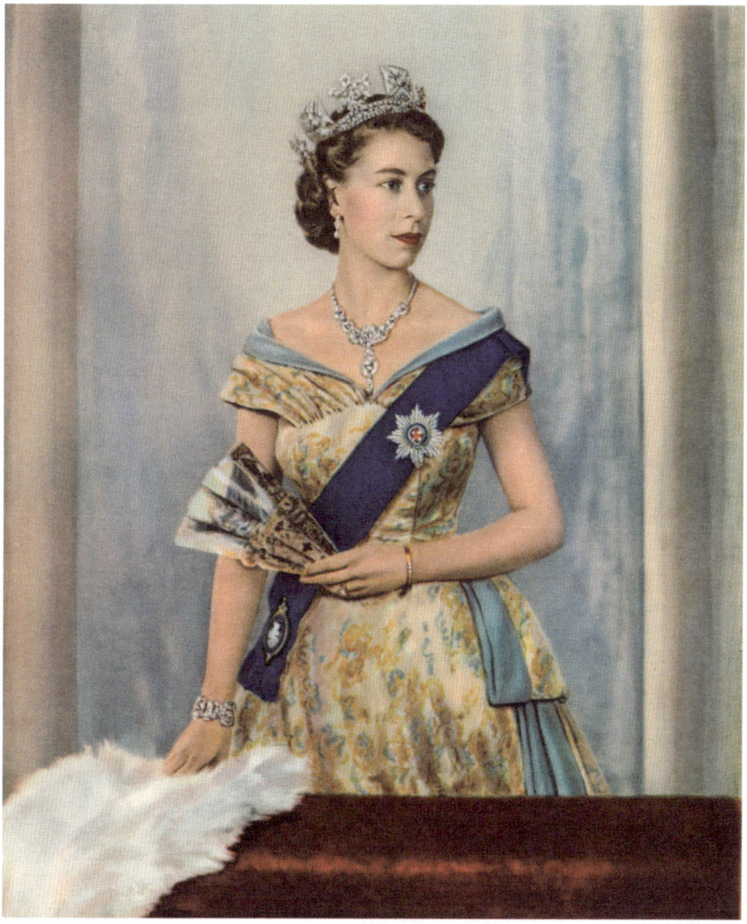

Her Majesty Queen Elizabeth II wearing the George IV State Diadem. She is guardian of the Royal Collection, holding it in trust for the next monarch.

never been a greater emphasis placed on conservation and care of the collection which now includes a computerised inventory of every item. Queen Elizabeth has travelled more than any monarch in our history and the Royal Collection now includes hundreds of gifts she has received on state visits.

In 1991, the National Maritime Museum, Greenwich, held *Henry VIII: A European Court in England*, an exhibition to celebrate the 500th anniversary of the king's birth. Elizabeth II loaned the exhibition fourteen Holbein drawings (including that of Nicholas Poyntz, whose love of Venetian glass was shared by Henry VIII) and Horenbout's miniature of Henry Fitzroy, as well as the clock supposedly given by Henry VIII to Anne Boleyn and later recovered for the Royal Collection by Queen Victoria. One of Henry's single-edged daggers was lent by the Royal Armouries, and a rare surviving piece from Henry's jewel house, the Royal Clock Salt, was lent by the Worshipful Company of Goldsmiths. For Henry it had functioned both as a table clock and a salt cellar, and of the eleven clock salts listed in his collection after his death is the only one that still survives.

The Queen's Gallery at Buckingham Palace mounted an exhibition in 2002 to mark the Golden Jubilee of Elizabeth II. It included an armorial tapestry panel from Henry VIII's collection, today at Hampton Court Palace, the hat badge depicting St George and the dragon, believed to have belonged to Henry VIII, and the Guido Mazzoni sculpture of a laughing child (possibly Henry VIII) dating to 1485.

The British Library held a major exhibition in 2009 to mark 500 years since Henry's accession called *Henry VIII: Man and Monarch*. It included items from the king's own library, 'books that he chose, read and annotated, and the documents and letters that he wrote'. In the accompanying catalogue, Henry was succinctly described as 'England's best-known king, with his six wives, his girth and his bloodthirstiness'. Perhaps an echo of the 'merciless prince', described by Sir Walter Raleigh in his somewhat ambitious *The Historie of the World*, 1614. Exhibitions containing items belonging to Henry VIII continue to attract high numbers of visitors as the fascination with this extraordinary monarch persists. It is fair to assume that the next major anniversary of this Tudor king will be met by an equally enthusiastic public, over whom Henry VIII continues to cast his spell.

But the Royal Collection also remains current. To celebrate the Diamond Jubilee of Elizabeth II in 2012, The Royal Collection Trust purchased four portrait prints of the queen by American pop artist Andy Warhol. They were based on photographs of Her Majesty taken in 1975 and released for the Silver Jubilee. The portraits are part of the royal edition of Warhol prints that are sprinkled with 'diamond dust', made from fine particles of crushed glass. And so, from Henry VIII to Her Majesty Queen Elizabeth II, the Royal Collection remains a testament to the collecting tradition of our British monarchs. It provides a record of their life and times as much in the twenty-first century as it did in the Tudor period of its founder.

APPENDIX

LIST OF ART WORKS AND TREASURES

1: Father and Son: Henry VII and Henry VIII

The Family of Henry VII with St George and the Dragon, Flemish school, 1503–09, oil on panel, Royal Collection, London. (Hampton Court Palace). RCIN 401228.

Portrait of Henry VII by an unknown Netherlandish artist, 1505, oil on panel, National Portrait Gallery, London. NPG 416.

Henry VIII when a young boy (?), Guido Mazzoni, 1498, painted and gilded terracotta, Royal Collection, London. RCIN 73197.

Wilton Diptych, French or English? *c.* 1395–99, Egg on oak, National Gallery, London, NG4451.

Tomb of Henry VII and Elizabeth of York, Pietro Torrigiano, 1509, black marble, copper gilt, Lady Chapel, Westminster Abbey.

Portrait of Thomas Cromwell, Hans Holbein the Younger, *c.* 1532, oil and tempera on oak panel, Frick Collection, New York.

2: From War to Diplomacy: The Early Years

The Battle of the Spurs, Flemish school, *c.* 1513, oil on canvas, (support, canvas/panel/str external), Royal Collection, London, (Hampton Court Palace). RCIN 406784.

Armour of Henry VIII, silvered and engraved, *c*. 1515, Royal Armouries, Tower of London.

The Field of the Cloth of Gold, English/Flemish school, *c*. 1545, oil on canvas, (support, canvas/panel/str external), Royal Collection, London, (Hampton Court Palace). RCIN 405794.

3: Painted Jewels: Miniatures and Stained Glass

Portrait of Henry VIII, Lucas Horenbout, 1525, Fitzwilliam Museum, Cambridge.

Henry VIII, Lucas Horenbout, *c*. 1526–27, watercolour on vellum laid on playing card, (ace of diamonds), Royal Collection, London, RCIN 420640.

Stained-glass windows of King Henry VIII and Katherine of Aragon, Unknown Netherlandish artist, 1536, St Margaret's church, Westminster.

4: The Break from Rome: Stoning the Pope

Portrait of Cardinal Thomas Wolsey, Sampson Strong, 1610–11, oil on panel, University of Oxford.

Henry VIII's Great Bible, 1539, Printed by Richard Grafton and Edward Whitchurch, British Library, London, System number: 000313335.

A Protestant Allegory, Girolamo da Treviso, 1538–44, oil on panel, Royal Collection, London, (Hampton Court Palace). RCIN 405748.

5: The King's Painter Hans Holbein at Home and Abroad

Self-portrait, Hans Holbein the Younger, 1542/43, coloured chalks on paper, Uffizi Gallery, Florence.

Mary, Duchess of Richmond and Somerset, Hans Holbein the Younger, 1532–33, black and coloured chalks, and ink on pale pink prepared paper, Royal Collection, London, RCIN 912212.

The Dance of Death by Hans Holbein the Younger is reproduced in full by Penguin Classics, ISBN-10: 0141396828, 2016.

Portrait of Desiderius Erasmus of Rotterdam with Renaissance Pilaster Hans Holbein the Younger, *c.* 1523, oil and tempera on panel, on loan from Longford Castle Collection, National Gallery, London, L 658.

Portrait of Sir Thomas More, Hans Holbein the Younger, 1527, oak panel, Frick Collection, New York.

John Fisher, Bishop of Rochester, Hans Holbein the Younger, 1532–34, black and coloured chalks, brown wash, pen and ink, brush and ink on pale pink prepared paper, Royal Collection, London, RCIN 912205.

Sir Henry Guildford, Hans Holbein the Younger, 1527, oil on oak panel, Royal Collection, London, RCIN 400046.

Portrait of Nicolaus Kratzer, Hans Holbein the Younger, 1528, Tempera on oak panel, Louvre, Paris.

'Noli Me Tangere' Hans Holbein the Younger, 1526–28, oil on oak panel, Royal Collection, London. (Windsor Castle). RCIN 400001.

The Artist's Family, Hans Holbein the Younger, 1528, oil on paper mounted on wood, Kunstmuseum, Basel.

Portrait of the Merchant George Gisze, Hans Holbein the Younger, 1532, oil on oak panel, Gemaldegalerie, Berlin.

Portrait of Hans of Antwerp, Hans Holbein the Younger, after 1532, oil on panel augmented with canvas, Royal Collection, London, RCIN 404443.

The Ambassadors, Hans Holbein the Younger, *c.* 1533, oil on oak panel, National Gallery, London, NG1314.

Portrait of Nicholas Bourbon, Hans Holbein the Younger, 1535, Black and coloured chalks, and pen and ink, Royal Collection, London, RCIN 912192.

Design for Jane Seymour's Cup, Hans Holbein the Younger *c.* 1536, ink and watercolour, Ashmolean Museum, Oxford.

Jane Seymour portrait, Hans Holbein the Younger, *c.* 1537, oil on panel, Kunsthistorisches Museum, Vienna.

Sir John Godsalve, Hans Holbein the Younger, *c.* 1532-4, black and red chalks, pen and ink, brush and ink, white heightening on pale pink prepared paper, Royal Collection, London, RCIN 912265.

Portrait of Anne of Cleves, Hans Holbein the Younger, 1539, oil and tempera on parchment mounted on canvas, Louvre, Paris.

6: Images of Heroes: The Whitehall Mural

Copy of the *Whitehall Mural*, Remigius van Leemput, *c.* 1667, oil on canvas, Royal Collection, London, (Hampton Court Palace), RCIN 405750.

Henry VIII, Hans Holbein the Younger, *c.* 1537, oil on panel, Museo Nacional Thyssen-Bornemisza, Madrid, Inv. No. 191 (1934.39).

Cartoon for the *Whitehall Mural*, Hans Holbein the Younger, 1536–37, ink and watercolour, National Portrait Gallery, London, NPG 4027.

King Edward VI, associated with Master John, *c.* 1547, oil on panel, National Portrait Gallery, London, NPG 5511.

King Edward VI, attributed to William Scrots, 1546–47, oil on panel, Royal Collection, London, RCIN 404441.

7: Magnificence and Propaganda: The Abraham Tapestries

The Story of Abraham, Pieter Coecke van Aelst, 1540–43, wool and silk with gilt metal wrapped thread, Royal Collection, London, (Hampton Court Palace), RCIN 1046.

8: Painting a Dynasty: The Family of Henry VIII

The Family of Henry VIII, English/Flemish school, *c.* 1545, oil on canvas, (support, canvas/panel/str external) Royal Collection, London, (Hampton Court Palace), RCIN 405796.

The Healing of the Lame Man (Acts 3: 1–8,) Raphael *c.* 1515–16, Cartoon for a tapestry, Victoria and Albert Museum, London.

Edward VI as a Child, Hans Holbein the Younger, 1539, oil on oak, National Gallery of Art, Washington D.C.

Family of Henry VIII with Will Somer, unknown artist, Duke of Buccleuch's collection at Boughton House, Northamptonshire. (Copy of an original panel painting, *c.* 1550s.)

9: Death and Memorial: The Body of Henry VIII

Henry VIII in old age, Cornelis Metsys, *c.* 1548, line engraving, National Portrait Gallery, London. NPG D24929.

Sketch of Henry VIII's vault in St George's Chapel, Alfred Young Nutt, 1888, St George's Chapel archives, SGC RBK H.386.

10: The Royal Collection: Henry VIII and Afterwards

The Royal Gold Cup, France *c.* 1370–80, British Museum, London.

The Clock Salt, Paris *c.* 1530–35, Worshipful Company of Goldsmiths, London.

Christina of Denmark, Duchess of Milan, Hans Holbein the Younger, 1538, oil on oak, National Gallery, London, NG 2475.

Coronation Anointing Spoon, twelfth century, silver gilt and freshwater pearls, British Crown Jewels, Tower of London, RNIC 31733.

Sir Nicholas Poyntz, Hans Holbein the Younger *c.* 1533/43, black and coloured chalks, and pen and ink on pale pink prepared paper, Royal Collection, London, (Queen Caroline's Closet, Kensington Palace), RCIN 912234.

Lady at the Virginals with a Gentleman, Johannes Vermeer, early 1660s, oil on canvas, Royal Collection, London, (Picture Gallery, Buckingham Palace), RCIN 405346.

The Diamond Diadem, Rundell Bridge & Rundell, 1820, diamonds, pearls, silver, gold, Royal Collection, London, (The Queen's Gallery, Buckingham Palace), RCIN 31702.

Anne Boleyn Clock, English, 1533, brass, silver gilt, wood, glass, lead, blued steel, Royal Collection, London, RCIN 30018.

Hat Badge with St George and the Dragon, Flemish, *c.* 1520, Royal Collection, London, RCIN 442208.

Henry Fitzroy, Duke of Richmond and Somerset, Lucas Horenbout, 1533–34, miniature in watercolour on vellum laid on card, Royal Collection, London, RCIN 420019.

Cullinan I and II Diamonds, the Sovereign's sceptre, RCIN 31712, and Imperial State Crown, RCIN 31701, British Crown Jewels, Royal Collection, London, (Tower of London).

Queen Mary's Dolls' House, Sir Edwin Lutyens, 1921–24, Royal Collection, London, (Windsor Castle), RCIN 231999.

Portrait of Her Majesty Queen Elizabeth II, Unknown artist, *c.* 1953, Her Majesty Queen Elizabeth II wearing the George IV State Diadem and the insignia of the Order of the Garter, Private Collection.

BIBLIOGRAPHY

Bolland, Charlotte and Cooper, Tarnya, *The Real Tudors: Kings and Queens Rediscovered*, National Portrait Gallery Publications, London, 2014.

Borman, Tracy, *Henry VIII and the Men who Made Him: The Secret History Behind the Tudor Throne*, Hodder & Stoughton, London, 2018.

Borman, Tracy, *The Private Lives of the Tudors*, Hodder & Stoughton, London, 2016.

Breiding, Dirk H., *The Function of Armour in Medieval and Renaissance Europe*, metmuseum.org/toah/hd_ufarm.htm, 2020.

Brewer, Clifford, *The Death of Kings*, Abson Books, London, 2000.

Brooke, Xanthe and Crombie, David, *Henry VIII Revealed: Holbein's Portrait and its Legacy*, Paul Holberton Publishing, London, 2003.

Campbell, Thomas P., 'Tapestry Quality in Tudor England', *Studies in Decorative Arts*, Vol. 3, No. 1, Winter 1995/6.

Campbell, Thomas P., *Tapestry in the Renaissance: Art & Magnificence*, The Metropolitan Museum of Art, New York, 2002.

Campbell, Thomas P., *Henry VIII and the Art of Majesty: Tapestries at the Tudor Court*, Yale University Press, New Haven, 2007.

Clarke, Siobhan and Collins, Linda, *The Tudors: The Crown, the Dynasty, the Golden Age*, Andre Deutsch, London, 2019.

Coombs, Katherine, *The Portrait Miniature in England*, V&A Publications, London, 1998.

Doren, Susan (Editor), *Henry VIII: Man & Monarch*, The British Library, London, 2009.
Foister, Susan, *Holbein in England*, Tate Publishing, London, 2006.
Hayward, Maria and Ward, Philip (Editors), *The Inventory of King Henry VIII: Volume II: Textiles and Dress 2*, Harvey Miller Publishers, London, 2012.
Hayward, Maria, 'Treasured Possessions: The Material World of Henry VIII', Southampton University, Unpublished essay.
Heard, Kate and Whittaker, Lucy, *The Northern Renaissance: Durer to Holbein*, Royal Collection Trust, London, 2013.
Hicks, Carola, *The King's Glass: A Story of Tudor Power and Secret Art*, Vintage Digital, London, 2010.
Hochstetler Meyer, Barbara, 'The First Tomb of Henry VII of England', *The Art Bulletin*, Vol. 58, No. 3, September 1976.
Lipscomb, Suzannah, *1536: The Year that Changed Henry VIII*, Lion Hudson, Chicago, 2009.
Lipscomb, Suzannah, 'All the King's Fools', *History Today*, Vol. 61, Issue 8, August 2011.
Lloyd, Christopher and Thurley, Simon, *Henry VIII: Images of a Tudor King*, Phaidon Press, London, 1990.
Loades, David, *Henry VIII: Court, Church and Conflict*, The National Archives, Kew, 2007.
Piper, David, *The English Face*, National Portrait Gallery Publications, London, 1978.
Reynolds, Graham, *English Portrait Miniatures*, Cambridge University Press, Cambridge, 1992.
Rider, Clare, *Henry VIII's Tomb*, Dean and Canon of St George's Chapel, Windsor, 2017–20.
Roberts, Jane (Editor), *Royal Treasures: A Golden Jubilee Celebration*, Royal Collection Enterprises Ltd, London, 2002.
Roberts, Jane (Editor), *Treasures: The Royal Collection*, Royal Collection Enterprises Ltd, London, 2008.
Scott, Jennifer, *The Royal Portrait: Image and Impact*, Royal Collection Enterprises Ltd, London, 2010.
Starkey, David (Editor), *Henry VIII: A European Court in England*, Collins & Brown, London, 1991.

Thurley, Simon, *The Royal Palaces of Tudor England: Architecture and Court Life*, Yale University Press, New Haven, 1993.
Thurley, Simon, *Hampton Court: A Social and Architectural History*, Yale University Press, New Haven, 2003.
Ward, Philip and Hawkyard, Alasdair, *The Inventory of King Henry VIII: The Transcript: 1*, Harvey Miller Publishers, London, 1998.
Weir, Alison, *Henry VIII: King and Court*, Vintage Digital, London, 2011.
Wilson, Derek, *Henry VIII: Reformer and Tyrant*, Constable and Robinson, London, 2009.
Wilson, Derek, *Hans Holbein: Portrait of an Unknown Man*, Vintage Digital, London, 2014.
Wyatt, Michael, *The Italian Encounter with Tudor England: A Cultural Politics of Translation*, Cambridge University Press, Cambridge, 2005.

You may also enjoy …

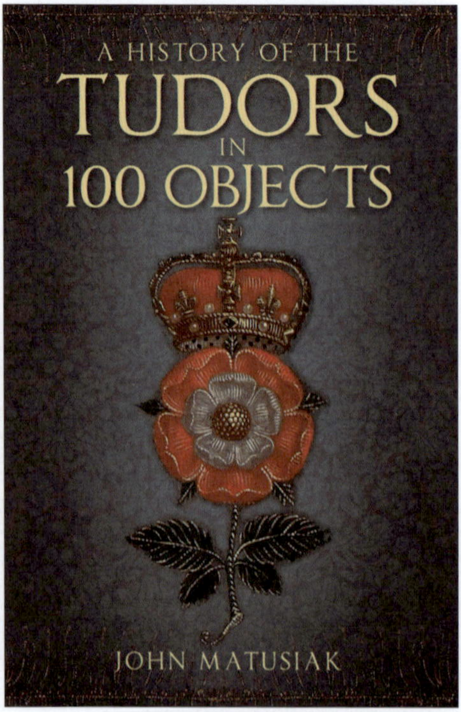

978 0 7509 9125 4

'Everything you wanted to know about the Merrie England of the Tudors and some things you probably did not. If the Tudors seem far removed, they are also curiously modern. They had spectacles and metal prosthetic arms, while a "fuming pot" was but a prototype Air Wick. Matusiak's mini essays accompanying the photographs are perfectly sculpted and the book is beautiful to hold.'

Charlotte Heathcote
The Sunday Express